THE ART OF DARKNESS

Deception and Urban Operations

Scott Gerwehr   Russell W. Glenn

Prepared for the United States Army

ARROYO CENTER

RAND

For more information on the RAND Arroyo Center, contact the Director of Operations, (310) 393-0411, extension 6500, or visit the Arroyo Center's Web site at http://www.rand.org/organization/ard/

Urban operations are a significant and enduring challenge by virtually any measure; but a battle on friendly urban terrain offers the weaker of combatants a chance to reduce the advantages of a stronger adversary. Something similar might be said of deception, historically a frequent resort of the underdog. Both the battle on friendly urban terrain and the employment of deception might be fairly characterized as *asymmetric strategies*, aimed at reducing an opponent's strengths and exposing his weaknesses. The admixture of these two strategies—when deception is employed in the urban environment—produces a powerful synergy. The research reported here was undertaken to gain a better understanding of the relationship between deception and the urban environment, first to explore the power of deception when employed *against* U.S. forces in urban operations, and second to evaluate the potential value of deception when used *by* U.S. forces in urban operations.

This research was undertaken for the Assistant Secretary of the Army (Acquisition, Logistics, and Technology) and was conducted in the Force Development and Technology Program of RAND's Arroyo Center. The Arroyo Center is a federally funded research and development center sponsored by the United States Army.

This study will be of interest to armed forces, law enforcement, or intelligence community personnel planning for or conducting operations and training in urban areas. Other governmental or nongovernmental agencies considering policies involving dedication of military, law enforcement, or intelligence assets in urban settings will likewise find herein material of value in determining the risks and potential costs or benefits of such policies.

CONTENTS

FIGURES

TABLES

SUMMARY

Though fraud in other activities may be detestable, in the management of war it is laudable and glorious, and he who overcomes the enemy by fraud is as much to be praised as he who does so by force.

—Niccolo Machiavelli, *Arte Della Guerra*

Urban operations remain an enduring challenge: they are fairly characterized as difficult, dangerous, complex, and manpower-intensive relative to other environments. If recent history is any guide, it is highly likely that U.S. forces will be called upon to operate in urban environments across a range of missions in the future. Recent research has noted that current doctrine, training, and technology are inadequate to support U.S. forces in future urban operations; many of the advantages held by U.S. forces are curbed or eliminated by the distinctive qualities of the urban environment. One area of potential vulnerability for U.S. forces is the need to face an adversary's use of deception (a likely part of an overall asymmetric strategy). Significantly, deception is also an area of great potential benefit if employed *by* U.S. forces as a core component of information operations (IO). The ingredients that make operating in urban terrain such a combustible mixture are well suited to facilitating deception on both the offensive and the defensive at all levels of war. Why is this so? While the methods and modes of deception remain relatively unchanging, deception is altered in form and abetted in function by the urban environment. This potentiating interrelationship between urban terrain and deception has six fundamental characteristics:

- The scope of deceptions is greater in the urban environment than in any other;
- The cacophonous "background noise" of urban environments hampers counterdeception faculties;
- Cities offer a rich trove of materials with which to conduct deception;
- Decisionmaking is generally worsened in urban environments relative to other environments;
- The presence and proximity of noncombatants complicate the intelligence picture at all operational levels;
- Urban clutter attenuates the leverage of technology.

These six factors represent a considerable hindrance when facing adversary deception in built-up areas, but also a potentially great help to U.S. forces conducting urban operations themselves.

Historically, deception has offered considerable leverage during urban operations. It may be both an enhancement to traditional military operations as well as an alternative to them. As such, it has a potential role in virtually every kind of U.S. and allied force mission. Although deception is recognized and respected as a potential source of great advantage for adversaries, it has probably been undervalued as a tool for friendly forces in doctrinal manuals and during training exercises, where it is often viewed as an ancillary activity. Moreover, doctrinal guidance pertaining to deception is often perfunctory boilerplate, even in the face of significant emerging technologies.

Deception may exploit technology, but it does not always have to depend on it, thus presenting a tool available to the urban combatant in both high- and low-technology contexts. For those who wish to contend on the urban battlefield of the 21st century, it would be advisable to more fully consider deception from both predictive (what will we see?) and prescriptive (what should we do?) vantage points. Prediction requires a careful review and analysis of historical precedent, as well as embracing deception as an important component of urban exercises and simulations. Prescription means improving the training, methods, and technologies for integrating deception more fully into the operational framework—at every level of war.

This document and the work it represents were made possible by the support and collaborative efforts of the entire RAND Arroyo Center urban operations team: Donna Betancourt, MAJ Geri Cherry, Sean Edwards, LTC Ernst Isensee, John Matsumura, Jamie Medby, and Dr. Randall Steeb. Also deserving of thanks are Ken Horn and David Chu of RAND's Arroyo Center, who provide leadership and a sure hand at the helm.

The authors have had numerous generative and fruitful discussions on deception with many people inside and outside RAND, all of whom merit thanks. The authors are grateful to Dr. Robert Anderson, Dr. Philip Antón, Matthew Feitshans, Dr. Philip Feldman, Kevin O'Connell, and Jeff Rothenberg for their perspicacity and exertions on behalf of this research. An early version of this research was briefed to the J8 Urban Working Group, and the authors are grateful to that body and to LTC Duane Schattle for the opportunity and feedback it brought.

The authors also recognize the professionalism and dedication of this document's reviewers. Robert Howe of RAND and LTG Ron Christmas (USMC, ret.) have generously offered their time and insights to improve this report. The authors also wish to thank Nikki Shacklett of RAND for her excellent editorial skills, and Pete Soriano and Ron Miller of RAND for their superb art and design efforts.

APC	Armored personnel carrier
ASU	Active service unit
C2	Command and control
COL	Colonel
COMINT	Communications intelligence
CONUS	Continental United States
FLN	Front de Libération Nationale
FM	Field manual
GIE	Global information environment
HUMINT	Human intelligence
IAD	Integrated air defenses
IDF	Israeli Defense Forces
IFF	Identification of friend or foe
IMINT	Imagery intelligence
IO	Information operations
IRA	Irish Republican Army

ISR	Intelligence, surveillance, reconnaissance
JFC	Joint force commander
JTF	Joint task force
JP	Joint publication
LTG	Lieutenant general
MAJ	Major
MASINT	Measurements and signatures intelligence
MCCD	Multispectral close-combat decoys
MCWP	Marine Corps warfighting publication
MIE	Military information environment
MTW	Major theater war
NCA	National command authorities
NEO	Noncombatant evacuation operation
NGO	Nongovernmental organization
NIR	Near infrared
OPSEC	Operational security
ROE	Rules of engagement
RPG	Rocket-propelled grenade
SAS	Special Air Service
SIGINT	Signals intelligence
SL	Sendero Luminoso [Shining Path]

Chapter One

INTRODUCTION

ZEGRA, Kosovo, June 23 [1999]. Local Serbs in civilian clothes opened fire tonight on a checkpoint run by United States Marines here, provoking a firefight that left one Serb dead and two others wounded, one severely, American officials here said.... [Commander of the 26th Marine Expeditionary Unit, COL Kenneth Glueck] said he believed that one or more Serbs had escaped. *"They faded into the crowd,"* he said.

—*The New York Times*, emphasis added

DJAKOVICA, Kosovo, June 27 [1999]. "It's exaggerated," a former senior allied official, who spoke to top European leaders in recent days, said of NATO's damage estimates. *"NATO hit a lot of dummy and deception targets.* It's an old Soviet ploy. Officials in Europe are very subdued. No one's pounding their chest over this." ... Careful reviews of cockpit video footage showed that some of the targets hit were not tanks or artillery batteries, but rather clever decoys made by the Serbs to fool pilots flying three or four miles up in the sky.

—*The New York Times*, emphasis added

THE PROBLEM

The urban environment has unique characteristics, making operations difficult and dangerous. Cities possess great numbers of noncombatants, are dense with vital infrastructures and important sociopolitical institutions, and are usually cluttered three-dimensional spaces that pose significant logistical and navigational challenges. It suffices to say that these and other characteristics conspire to create a daunting environment for U.S. forces. The World War II–

era urban combat policy for U.S. forces involved clearing and holding urban areas on a room-by-room and building-by-building basis. This tends to be a bloody, expensive, disorienting, time-consuming, and manpower-intensive business—one that is increasingly deficient in the complex post–Cold War world. U.S. and allied forces are called on today to perform a range of missions in urban environments, for example in stability and support missions. Some missions are amenable to the WWII urban combat policy, but many others are not. Moreover, most of these missions are on foreign soil, presenting U.S. forces with the prospect of operating amid alien and perhaps unfriendly noncombatants in unfamiliar and complex terrain. This raises a trenchant point: the possibility that an overmatched adversary confronting the United States will invite battle in their own urban environment as part of an *asymmetric strategy*. Such a strategy seeks to apply one's strength to an adversary's perceived weaknesses, knowing that a strength-on-strength approach would be less profitable. Putting a strong opponent into unfamiliar and complex territory, blunting his edges in information gathering and command and control, and setting him among an unfriendly population are all tactics that embody asymmetric thinking.

A brief demonstration of the asymmetric approach to warfighting might be useful. Per the Biblical parable, consider some hypothetical options available to David in facing Goliath:

1. Hand-to-hand combat in open ground

2. Hand-to-hand combat in dense woods, where Goliath has difficulty maneuvering

3. David employs a missile weapon, while Goliath employs a hand-to-hand weapon

4. David sneaks up on Goliath while the latter is sleeping and stabs him

Option 1 would be a symmetric approach: David's strength versus Goliath's strength. Options 2–4 would be examples of asymmetric approaches. In Option 2, Goliath's advantages are offset to some degree by hindering terrain. In Options 3 and 4, David avoids Goliath's strengths altogether and strikes at his weaknesses.

The widely analyzed, canonical example of the asymmetric approach in high-intensity conflict is the battle for Stalingrad in 1942, where Soviet forces reduced German advantages in air power and artillery and forced a brutal fight in urban terrain well known to the Soviets. Low-intensity urban campaigns are even more common but less well studied. At present, the United States is a force-projection power and thus far more likely to face adversaries on their home ground than the reverse. Furthermore, the United States is arguably the foremost military power in the world, driving opponents to seek asymmetric strategies should they need to contend with the United States. As noted above, inviting battle on friendly urban terrain is one possible asymmetric approach to warfighting. It is no surprise, therefore, that the U.S. armed forces have selected a doctrine of "urban avoidance" in the post–World War II world.

Unfortunately, "urban avoidance" (or its kin, "siege warfare") may be less tenable than the U.S. armed forces have come to expect. Global trends and national security imperatives converge on the urban battlefields of the future. It seems certain that U.S. joint forces will participate in future urban operations, whether unilaterally or in coalition—for example, in humanitarian relief or, at the other end of the spectrum, in full-scale warfighting. Recent operations in Panama, Haiti, Somalia, and Bosnia amply illustrate the point. It is also worth noting that, with exceptions like the employment of troops in Detroit in 1965 and Los Angeles in 1992, most instances of urban operations for U.S. forces since World War II involved force projection, and all have had restrictive rules of engagement (ROE) for noncombatants and their infrastructure to some degree or another. While much is being done to improve the auspices for future urban operations, there remain significant shortcomings in doctrine, training, and technologies to ensure mission accomplishment and force protection in such engagements. The need for U.S. forces to operate outside of the continental United States (CONUS), the presence of restrictive ROE, and the perceived intolerance of the U.S. public to casualties necessitate the development of better means and methods for operating in urban terrain.

THE GOALS OF THIS REPORT

This analysis focuses upon a single area of great importance in urban operations: deception. Consider again the asymmetrically minded strategist. One method of neutralizing an opponent's strengths (in say, air power and artillery) is to do battle in friendly urban terrain. Another is *to cause the opponent to misapply his strengths.* Deception offers the best method for achieving this effect. Deception used by adversaries represents a potent and enduring challenge to U.S. forces, as the recent Balkan air war ably demonstrates. But why should opponents possess exclusive rights to clever asymmetric strategies? Deception used by friendly forces represents a very effective force multiplier.

This monograph is therefore concerned with two primary points: first, how and to what effect future adversaries might attempt to deceive U.S. forces during urban operations, and second, how and to what effect U.S. forces might employ deception to accomplish their objectives in those same urban operations. It is *not* our contention that the use of deception is automatically decisive, or that it is cost or risk free. However, an examination of relevant history and a careful consideration of the nature of the urban environment reveals this to be fertile ground if properly cultivated, and our adversaries will certainly reap such a harvest if we do not. This analysis will concentrate on the relationship between military deception and the singular nature of the urban environment, formulating hypotheses on how they interact (and appropriating examples from the historical record where illustrative). Our hypotheses shall serve as a foundation for any prescriptions we may make, whether in experimentation, design, training, technological improvement, or the like.

Is current U.S. doctrine for urban operations fully leveraging deception for operational and tactical advantage? We seek here to provoke consideration of deception as a potent and underappreciated instrument, and to spark debate as to whether current considerations of deception are sufficient. We wish to assess the utility of deception in U.S. and allied urban operations, and also to do the same for adversaries in those same arenas. Moreover, our prescriptions here should set the stage for the creation of a "toolbox" of deceptions and methods for employing them in future urban operations.

Succinctly put, the goals of this monograph are twofold: to heighten awareness of the important role deception can play *for both friendly and hostile forces* in urban operations, and to create a solid analytical foundation for modification of current doctrine, training, and technology requirements.

THE METHODOLOGY

We approach this topic in three sections.

First, we turn our attention to the urban environment, examining its key characteristics and how operations are conducted within built-up areas. The outcome of this examination should be a profile of the challenges and pitfalls of urban operations, as distinct from those of other environments.

Second, we define deception and how it is employed, describing its goals, process, means, and hazards. An important answer should emerge from this discussion: whether and which of the prerequisites and facilitators of deception are found in the urban operations milieu.

Finally, we study the interrelationship of deception and urban operations, considering whether and how urban terrain affects deception, making use of historical examples where relevant and illuminating.

This analysis is concerned exclusively with deception, and it will touch only briefly on other important components of information operations (e.g., psychological operations). While these topics are no less important, they will be discussed only where directly relevant to this analysis.

THE SOURCE MATERIALS

We make use of both formal pronouncements of U.S. doctrine (joint and service publications) as well as less official settings for doctrinal discussion (working groups and the like). We have also made extensive use of historical accounts and lessons learned from a variety of recent military engagements, where apt. These include many of the well-documented high-intensity urban operations in the past fifty years, such as

- Stalingrad, Ortona, Aachen, Berlin, Manila (1942–1945)
- Seoul (1950)
- Hue (1968)
- Suez City (1973)
- Panama City (1989)
- Mogadishu (1993)
- Grozny (1995)

In addition, where possible we have drawn from more marginal (but equally important) primary sources: writings and interviews of terrorists, insurgents, criminals, and the like. Many of these individuals have directly participated in urban conflicts (often in opposition to U.S. or allied forces) and have written or spoken of their experiences. While not exhaustive, the list of sources includes

- Irgun (Israel, 1946–1948)
- Provisional Irish Republican Army (United Kingdom, 1916–1999)
- Front de Libération Nationale (Algeria, 1956–1962)
- Sendero Luminoso (Peru, 1980–1999)
- 2nd-of-June and Red Army Faction (Germany, 1968–1972)

Detailed historical case studies are beyond the scope of this report; for those interested we include a complete bibliography.

Chapter Two

URBAN TERRAIN AND URBAN OPERATIONS

WHAT IS THE NATURE OF URBAN TERRAIN?

We will use the terms "urban environment," "urban terrain," and "built-up areas" interchangeably. A useful working definition of these terms, drawn from Army FM 90-10-1, is the following:

> A concentration of structures, facilities, and people that forms the economic and cultural focus for the surrounding area. The four categories of built-up areas are large cities, towns and small cities, villages, and strip areas.

Note that the definition explicitly includes the *population* of the terrain, one of several features unique to the urban environment that affect operations. Urban areas are centers of social, financial, and political importance in a country, and they usually serve as regional nodes for transportation, communication, and industry. The significance of such areas suggests that they will be bitterly contested should strife overtake the region. History has borne out this supposition, as a review of major battles during the 20th century reveals. Interestingly, the words of West German terrorist Michael Baumann attest to the importance that so many insurgencies likewise place upon the urban arena:

> [W]hat's needed is a vanguard in the metropolis that declares its solidarity with the liberation movements of the third world. *Since it lives in the head of the monster, it can do the greatest damage there.* (Baumann, 1975, p. 46, emphasis added.)

A detailed discussion of the morphology of the urban environment—urban zone types, building materials, construction methods, weapons effects, and the like—is beyond the scope of this report. For an excellent treatment of these important issues, see Ellefsen (1987).

HOW IS URBAN TERRAIN DISTINCT FROM OTHER TYPES OF TERRAIN?

The urban environment possesses unique qualities. Unsurprisingly, these qualities figure prominently in the challenge to forces wishing to operate in built-up areas. As noted by Ellefsen (1987, p. 12),

> Urban terrain, being a man-made environment, is composed of angular forms, the like of which occurs only rarely in non-urban terrain. Not only are these forms angular in planimetric pattern (as a grid street pattern), but in the third dimension as well. Verticality becomes of great importance, for this not only creates extremely difficult barriers to assault, but provides the defense with a man-made form of "high-ground." A large city provides several planes of "urban high ground" and, in many instances, a subterranean level in addition.

But the unique *physical* aspects of urban terrain are only half of the equation; the *human* factor is just as important. As noted in the doctrinal definition above, human beings populate urban terrain in great numbers—vastly more so than any other type of operating environment. The presence of large numbers of noncombatants and their interaction with friendly or hostile forces play a critical role in the outcomes of urban operations.

A comparison of the urban environment with other operating environments, focused upon features key to operations of many sorts, appears in Table 1. The great difficulty of operating in urban environments can be ascribed in large part to the two factors noted above: the physical uniqueness of urban terrain and the presence of a large noncombatant population.

Importantly, the force in possession of a city, with time to prepare and/or be supported by a friendly noncombatant population, often finds some of these difficulties ameliorated. Not so for the outsider. For example, the Egyptian defenders of Suez City in 1973 were able to

Table 1

Some Differences Between Urban and Other Types of Terrain

	Urban	Desert	Jungle	Mountain
Number of noncombatants	High	Low	Low	Low
Amount of valuable infrastructure	High	Low	Low	Low
Presence of multidimensional battlespace	Yes	No	Some	Yes
Restrictive rules of engagement	Yes	No	No	No
Detection, observation, engagement ranges	Short	Long	Short	Medium
Avenues of approach	Many	Many	Few	Few
Freedom of movement and maneuver—mech forces	Low	High	Low	Medium
Communications functionality	Degraded	Normal	Normal	Degraded
Logistical requirements	High	High	Medium	Medium

rely upon friendly noncombatants as couriers when radio and other methods of communication failed. The Israeli forces in this case had no such option. This is the essence of *urban battle as an asymmetric strategy.* As Table 1 notes in simplified fashion, many faculties and capabilities are diminished while operating in the city, but this burden is borne disproportionately by the outsider. Recalling our illustrative parable: should David choose to fight amongst dense woods instead of open ground, he too will be hampered but Goliath will be more so, and thus the overall disparity between them is reduced.

A demonstration of this principle can be seen in the Russian experience in the January 1995 battle for Grozny:

> The Chechens were at a huge advantage fighting on home ground in a city most knew from childhood. They worked mostly at night, laying mines and carrying supplies and ammunition to forward positions. Their mobility was their great strength. Using back alleys and the sewers, slipping through basements and destroyed buildings, they danced around the Russians, who often clung to the dubious safety of their armored vehicles. (Gall and De Waal, 1998, p. 206.)

While the Chechens surely found crawling through sewers and operating at night to be difficult, it was far more onerous for the Russians. The Chechens used the urban battlefield as we suggested David might have used dense woods: to offset Russian advantages and exploit Russian weaknesses.

As an aside, consider what this suggests about the application of deception in urban terrain. Deception is by itself an asymmetric approach to warfighting: tricking the opponent into misapplying his strengths and revealing his weaknesses. It is frequently (though certainly not exclusively) used by Davids against prospective Goliaths, as Clausewitz (1873) noted:

> The weaker the forces that are at the disposal of the supreme commander, the more appealing the use of cunning becomes.

The use of *deception in urban terrain,* therefore, is actually two separate asymmetric strategies folded into one. Will this have a cumulative effect? A synergistic one? We will keep these questions in mind as we proceed in our analysis.

WHAT KINDS OF OPERATIONS ARE PERFORMED IN URBAN TERRAIN?

U.S. Army doctrine has heretofore advocated avoiding operations in urban terrain when possible, reflecting an awareness of the challenges posed by such an environment. A 1986 report by the Defense Science Board opined that "avoiding urban involvements is by far the wisest course." However, current Army and Marine Corps doctrine asserts that operations to isolate, capture, neutralize, or stabilize urban terrain will be performed when

1. Political or humanitarian concerns demand;

2. Strategic, operational, or tactical advantages are likely to be gained;

3. Avoiding the built-up area poses a threat to friendly interests.

These disparate "causes" for urban operations suggest immediately the widely varying types of urban operations U.S. forces may be called upon to perform. In general terms, these missions include the following:

- **Special operations.** These include hostage rescue, reconnaissance, direct action, and other missions involving small, well-trained units operating usually in hostile environments.

- **Peace support or stabilization.** Whether unilaterally or in coalition, these missions usually occur in permissive or semipermissive environments and frequently entail humanitarian and medical assistance, disaster relief, counterinsurgency, policing of an accord, or separating hostile groups. As part of foreign internal assistance, the United States has often contributed forces to help an ally combat terrorism or guerrilla activity; and historically, urban centers figure prominently in insurgent campaigns.

- **Isolation, cordon, denial.** If an important piece of urban terrain is controlled by hostile defenders but its capture is not of immediate necessity, U.S. forces may be required to encircle it. This could be preparatory to a subsequent attack, or it may be done to neutralize the terrain while it is bypassed by other friendly forces. In a related circumstance, if an important piece of built-up terrain is not yet in the grip of an adversary, friendly forces may wish to "deny" it to him.

- **Attack to capture or control.** In a full-scale conflict, U.S. forces may be required to seize or dominate urban terrain from hostile defenders who may or may not have prepared the area. Such actions may be hasty or deliberate.

- **Mobile or static defense.** While the United States and its allies are predominately force-projection powers, there could well be cases demanding that U.S. forces prepare and defend a city against an imminent attack (e.g., Seoul). As with offensive actions, these defensive moves may be hasty or deliberate.

HOW DOES URBAN TERRAIN AFFECT THOSE OPERATIONS?

As described above, the city environment can create numerous operational difficulties that make the invitation to battle on urban terrain a well-known asymmetric strategy. The key difficulties (distilled from Army FM 90-10-1, *An Infantryman's Guide to Combat in Built-Up Areas* (with Change 1), and Marine Corps Warfighting Publication 3-35.3, *Military Operations on Urbanized Terrain*) are noted below.

Noncombatants and their attendant infrastructure are significantly present, necessitating rules of engagement (ROE). Any operation in urban terrain is virtually guaranteed to have large numbers of non-combatants in the immediate vicinity, and U.S. policy clearly disallows large numbers of civilian casualties in most cases. Given civilian dependence upon power, water, and other types of supporting infrastructure (this includes sites of cultural importance), destruction of these facilities is also generally unacceptable. Note also that populations of cities tend to be heterogeneous, including the presence of regional and international groups (Red Cross, UN peacekeepers, foreign embassies, etc.). Moreover, built-up terrain usually contains a wealth of resources (food, fuel, vehicles, etc.) desirable to the adversary or to opportunist looters. Lastly, the relationship of combatants to the indigenous noncombatants is critical and may weigh heavily in the outcome of operations at all levels of war. As noted by Bell (1997, p. 375),

> A great strength for the IRA had been created by the segregated housing pattern that produced Catholic Ghettos: some bright, new housing estates, others warrens of little streets and tiny brick houses. With well-defined boundaries they were closed communities of friends and neighbors and an alien presence was noted and reported at once; moreover, the increasingly aggressive searches and sweeps of the British Army after August [1971] guaranteed that the neighbors would remain friends, would supply an urban safe-base for the Active Service Units recruited from the area.

This also suggests an important point that we shall revisit later: while many sources of intelligence (imagery, communications intercepts, etc.) may be degraded in built-up areas, sources of human intelligence may multiply, particularly for the combatant with friendly ties to the local populace.

The battlespace is three-dimensional, with subterranean, surface, and building/rooftop features, all of military significance. Operations can and will occur simultaneously in and around all of these elements. The potential for infiltration/exfiltration and flanking maneuvers is thus greatly enhanced, particularly when coupled with the presence of multiple avenues of approach at each of the subterranean, surface, and building/rooftop levels. As Ellefsen notes (1987, p. 12),

> The multiplication of surface space in the form of multistory buildings, means that even though the total area of cities is not very great, the aggregate total surface space (the floor area) on which combat could occur is several times greater than the surface space shown on a map and represents a sizable area when totaled.

Buildings and structures figure prominently in observation, fire, and movement. As noted in MCWP 3-35.3, "buildings provide cover and concealment; limit or increase fields of observation and fire; and canalize, restrict, or block movement of forces, especially mechanized forces." Buildings can serve as ready-made fortifications, making clearing operations difficult and time-consuming. The battle for Hue City is a prime example of this, wherein North Vietnamese army forces created strongpoints using multistory buildings and their courtyards (Christmas, 1977). Moreover, the size and number of buildings in built-up areas greatly increases manpower requirements for seizing, clearing and holding portions of urban terrain.

Command and control (C2) is complex and chaotic, presenting significant difficulties to combatant commanders. Small units are usually the central players in urban conflict, with control sometimes devolving all the way down to squad level. Communications and intelligence—two of the most critical capabilities in operations—are frequently degraded (regarding the latter, HUMINT may be an exception, as noted above). Identification of friend or foe (IFF) is a nontrivial challenge; units frequently become disoriented and confused. Operational tempo is usually high (particularly in combat missions), substantially reducing the time frame of decisionmaking. The poor decisions that sometimes result can lead to a catastrophic worsening of an already difficult problem, as noted by McLaurin and Snider (1982, p. 20) in their discussion of the fighting in Suez City during the 1973 Arab-Israeli conflict:

> The result of the surprise at the Arba'in Junction was disastrous for the attacking IDF [Israeli Defense Forces]. Virtually all the tank commanders in the lead battalion were wounded or killed, with only four remaining officers left to carry out their functions. Some

of the tanks and APCs were unable to move, effectively blocking the road for others. Command and control were destroyed as a result of the simultaneous loss of almost all tank commanders, widespread injury to communications personnel, and the overloading of all tactical radio nets with appeals for assistance. Tanks and APCs veered into side streets in which many were trapped and could not escape.

The urban environment promotes stressful, high-intensity close combat, leading to significant logistical and medical challenges. Urban engagements occur mostly at close range (100 meters or less), involve tremendous expenditures of supply, and are particularly bloody and time-consuming. The battlespace features fire from all directions, plus the aforementioned degradation of C2 and high operational tempo, which can lead to high levels of duress and casualties. Consider just one example from the January 1995 fighting in Grozny, described by Gall and De Waal (1998, p. 206):

> [Photographer Patrick] Chauvel was with a group of Chechen fighters sloshing through the city's sewers, one of the safest ways to cut through the city on the way to an ambush, when the commander in front pushed him down and opened fire into the darkness. A furious gun battle lit up the pitch-black tunnel, as half a dozen rifles opened up and bullets ricocheted off the roof, killing the man behind Chauvel. They had walked slap into a Russian patrol group.

This type of sudden, bloody, close-in fighting is prevalent in urban operations; indeed, it is the historical hallmark of urban operations.

This discussion raises an interesting question: do the factors that make invitation to urban battle an asymmetric strategy have any relationship to deception? In fact, as we proceed in our analysis, it shall become clear that many of the key characteristics of urban operations, noted above, are prerequisites and facilitators of deception.

Chapter Three

DECEPTION

All warfare is based upon deception.

—Sun Tzu, *The Art of War*

WHAT IS DECEPTION? WHAT IS MILITARY DECEPTION?

Deception, the employment of trickery or guile, is equal parts art and science. It is typically defined as "causing another to believe what is not true; to mislead or ensnare" (Webster's, 1999). Deception aims to *deliberately induce misperception in another.* Deception is a deliberate enterprise; it is not the result of chance, nor the by-product of another endeavor (McCleskey, 1991). Whaley (1982, p. 188) has defined deception as "information designed to manipulate the behavior of others by inducing them to accept a false or distorted presentation of their environment—physical, social, or political." It is ubiquitous and enduring in human affairs, and equally prevalent in the predator-prey relationships of the plant and animal kingdoms. Note that while we define *human* deception as requiring *deliberation,* this is not the case in the animal or plant kingdoms. Rather than ascribe intentions to other species, we shall simply aver that deception in animals and plants is any act or instrument whereby an individual organism induces a misperception in another. Deceptions may therefore include the lure of the angler fish; the brood mimicry of the cuckoo's egg; the diverting eyespots of the moth's wing; the camouflage of the trapdoor spider's ambush; and the feigned injury of the parent duck.

A closer look at animal biology and behavior reveals important principles of deception, tabulated below (drawn from Wickler, 1968; Dawkins and Krebs, 1978, 1979; Slatkin and Maynard Smith, 1979; Erichsen, Krebs, and Houston, 1980; and Owen, 1980).

- **Species of all types use deception.** Deception (as defined previously) is present in virtually every branch of the evolutionary tree (vertebrates and invertebrates alike). Fish, reptiles, birds, mammals: every category of animal life (and a great many plants) employs deception.

- **Many types of deception are employed in nature (camouflage, concealment, diversion, conditioning/exploit, mimicry).** Not only are many types of deception used, but within a single type of deception—camouflage, for example—deception is polymorphic. That is to say, camouflage (known in biology as "crypsis") can be as simple as green skin coloration for a background of foliage, or as complex as a nest whose shape, emissions, and entryways are all disguised by local materials (dirt, twigs, stones, etc.).

- **Every environment supports deception in at least one inhabitant of its ecosystem, and usually by many.** Deception is present in every environment supporting life (whether terrestrial, aquatic, or airborne): from desolate Arctic wastes to richly populated equatorial jungles.

- **Deception is used by both predators (offensively) and prey (defensively).** Deception in nature is used both to acquire dinner and to avoid becoming dinner—it is among the best methods for both successfully preying and escaping predation (as opposed to speed or armor, for example). The extremely venomous boomslang snake hunts the well-camouflaged chameleon not by evolving better sensors, but by employing its own excellent camouflage techniques. The chameleon's crypsis is far less effective while it moves, and if it doesn't see the boomslang, it moves.

- **A single species can use deception in both ways.** The same methods a given species uses to facilitate predation are often applied with equal effectiveness by that species to escape predation. Many species of small insects and spiders bear a striking resemblance to ants, which allows both protection from predators uninterested in ants as well as unhindered access to ant colonies where they may scavenge. Interestingly, this type of mimicry is also performed using chemical signature molecules as a "passcode-scent" quite apart from physical appearance.

- **Even minor applications of deception can confer selective advantage.** Experimental data show that even lesser deceptive techniques provide measurable benefits. For example, insects with even slight amounts of crypsis are less likely to be preyed upon by blue jays.

- **Deception is more effective in some environments than others.** Experimental data show that deceptive techniques vary in their effectiveness by environment. Where animal density is high, crypsis offers greater protection from predation (suggesting reasonably that we will see disguise to be more effective among city crowds than in desert wastes).

These latter two principles suggest critical experiments that should be performed in gauging military applications of deception, and we shall return to this topic later on.

Humans, like animals, must make decisions in order to survive. Decisionmakers rely upon their assessment of other actors' interests, intentions, and capabilities, as well as an assessment of the environment or context within which the action takes place. These assessments—or *perceptions*—engender policy preferences and galvanize action. It is incumbent upon decisionmakers to form *accurate* perceptions if they are to successfully navigate the shoals of circumstance; history is famously littered with the ruin of those who failed to do so. For example, the name of Neville Chamberlain, the British Prime Minister who "appeased" Hitler at Munich, is nearly synonymous with catastrophic misperception (though not *necessarily* as a result of German deception). Forming accurate perceptions is a challenge even under favorable circumstances. These latter circumstances might include situations with clear and unambiguous communication between parties, or extensive preparation and rehearsal for a particular turn of events. Unfavorable circumstances might include occasions when events are unfolding at a very fast pace, or when the background "noise" of contradictory opinions interferes with the accurate gauging of an actor's intentions. Within these "unfavorable" circumstances is a subset in which one or more parties attempts to *deceive* the other(s). Such deception might be explicit or implied, may involve concealing what is true or displaying what is false, or a combination of both. As noted above, the aim of deception is to produce an inaccurate assessment, or *misperception*, in the mind of the target that the deceiver can then exploit.

In the domain of conflict and war, deception is widely perceived to be both applicable and valuable, from the construction of decoys that draw enemy fire to the use of a feint to deflect enemy attention away from a major attack. Military deception aims to *deliberately induce misperception in another for tactical, operational, or strategic advantage.* Deception, like other components of information operations (IO), has "as its ultimate target the human decision making process" (Joint Pub 3-13, *Joint Doctrine for Information Operations*). Recent U.S. military doctrine (Army Field Manual 101-5-1, *Operational Terms and Graphics;* Joint Pub 3-58, *Joint Doctrine for Military Deception;* and Army Field Manual 90-2, *Battlefield Deception*) defines military deception as

> measures taken to deliberately mislead adversary decision-makers about friendly capabilities, intentions or operations in ways which may be exploited by friendly forces.

In this monograph we shall broaden this definition slightly, replacing the word "adversary" with the word "relevant," operating from the premise that deceptions targeted against noncombatants may also play an important role in military operations. This is consonant with the current doctrine relating to information operations, into which deception is bundled, and which are defined by U.S. Army Field Manual 100-6 (*Information Operations*) as

> continuous military operations within the Military Information Environment (MIE) that enable, enhance, and protect the friendly force's ability to collect, process, and act upon information to achieve an advantage across the full range of military operations; IO include interacting with the Global Information Environment (GIE) and exploiting or denying an adversary's information and decision capabilities.

The presence of large numbers of noncombatants is one of the key features distinguishing the urban from other environments, as noted in the previous chapter. Effects upon the GIE—which are defined to be persons, information, and information systems *outside* the control of the National Command Authorities (NCA)—may be as militarily significant as effects upon the MIE, defined to be persons, information, and information systems *within* the purview of the NCA. The GIE includes governmental and nongovernmental actors, social and cultural elements, and innumerable local, regional, and transnational infrastructures. Historical accounts amply document the useful employment of deception in all environments, supported by a broad range of technologies and aimed at both noncombatants (journalists, clerics, civilian leadership, etc.) as well as principals in enemy command structures (generals, intelligence analysts, pilots, etc.). As defined above, deception (as part of information operations) can be valuable in both the offensive and defensive roles; it is clear that an adversary may utilize deception similarly.

A note on terminology: throughout the foreign policy, intelligence, and defense communities—and over time—various definitions and formulations of deception have been proposed. They include "denial and deception," "concealment, camouflage, and deception," "perceptions management," and so on. Here we group them all under a single aegis with the definition outlined above. If an operation, a technique, or measure has as its goal the deliberate purveyance of falsehood to another in order to aid friendly interests, we call it deception. As noted above, this may take the form of hiding things, revealing things, or a combination of the two; for the purposes of this monograph, it is all deception. Thus camouflage (which aims to conceal) is related to decoys (which aim to reveal). Deception is an integral component of information operations, themselves a vital component of overall operational art; it follows that the framework developed for employing information operations governs using deception as well.

WHAT WOULD DECEPTION BE USED FOR?

I make the enemy see my strengths as weaknesses and my weaknesses as strengths while I cause his strengths to become weaknesses and discover where he is not strong.

—Sun Tzu, *The Art of War*

As a component of both offensive and defensive IO, deception is used to adversely affect an opponent's decisionmaking processes, most often to influence or degrade enemy command and control (C2). For example, deception may promote friendly intelligence, surveillance, and reconnaissance (ISR) activities; may thwart ISR in an adversary; may degrade enemy cohesion and C2; may enhance force protection and survivability; and may create opportunities to engage and even surprise the enemy. These effects could also be gained against an individual enemy soldier in a low-intensity urban insurgency, as described by IRA operative Eamon Collins (1997, p. 124):

> [T]he other [bomb] had been built into the dashboard of a brown Mark 4 Cortina, which would be used as the getaway car. It would be abandoned with the aim of attracting a nosy bomb-disposal squad officer or policeman. If the glove compartment was opened, an electrical circuit would be completed which would detonate ten pounds of high explosives. Another [Active Service Unit] had used a similar trick some time earlier. A bomb-disposal officer had cut out the windscreen of the suspicious car in order to avoid opening the doors; then he had leaned in and opened the glove compartment . . .

Deception may just as readily be employed against an entire enemy army in a high-intensity, major theater urban conflict, as in the case of the Chechens' defense of Grozny, observed by Anatol Lieven (1998, p. 109):

> [T]he lack of obvious barricades and tank traps made [us] think that the Chechens would put up only a symbolic fight in the city. But . . . they were much better tacticians than that.

Alternatively, deception could be applied against anyone at all unfriendly to the deceiver. As Monmonier describes (1996, p. 117), one form of deception useful at all levels of war is disinformation directed at mapping/navigating skills:

> Soviet cartographic disinformation affected all [publicly available] maps of urban areas. Detailed street maps of Moscow and other Soviet cities often failed to identify principal thoroughfares and usually omitted a scale, so that distances were difficult to estimate. Although local citizens were well aware of its presence, Soviet street

maps of Moscow suppressed the imposing KGB building on Dzerzhinski square, as well as other important buildings.

The principles and practice of deception remain the same in all of the preceding examples, as will be described below. Furthermore, deception has comparable effects at all levels of war—the creation of one or more prejudicial misperceptions in the mind of the target—differing mainly in scale and particulars.

How does deception accomplish these ambitious objectives? As noted above, deception creates misperceptions—the sorts of which are virtually infinite. However, a few general categories serve to encompass a broad range of possibilities. Deception may

- Purposefully condition the target to a pattern of friendly behavior;

- Divert the target's attention from friendly assets;

- Draw the target's attention to a particular time and place;

- Hide the presence or absence of activity from the target;

- Advertise strength or weakness as their respective opposites;

- Confuse or overload the target's intelligence apparatus;

- Disguise friendly forces as neutrals or even members of the enemy's force.

Consider the first category: This venerable ploy is colloquially known as a "crying wolf" tactic, and it relies upon the desensitizing effects of repetition to diminish a target's readiness or alertness. Specifically, the misperceptions created in the target's mind are, first, *that friendly activities follow a consistent, uniform course;* second, *that departure from the pattern (i.e., surprise) is unlikely;* and third, *that jeopardy is reduced overall by the predictability of these activities.* Two historical examples will serve to illustrate this brand of ruse (and simultaneously demonstrate the enduring nature of deception):

- In 1973 AD, Egyptian forces assaulting the Bar-Lev line in Suez City surprised Israeli forces and scored great offensive gains in the opening hours of the Yom Kippur War. Egyptian forces had staged a number of deceptive operations to hoodwink Israeli intelligence, and among these were back-and-forth movements of men and materiel to potential crossing points. Troops were moved to the canal, tank ramps were constructed, and openings were made in the canal ramparts, yet each time there was a flurry of activity there was also a subsequent "standing down" of Egyptian forces. These repetitive events (what Richard Betts calls "alert fatigue") lulled Israeli observers into a less-vigilant state which, coupled with poor Israeli analysis and self-deception, led to near catastrophe. (Drawn from Betts, 1983, and Dunnigan and Nofi, 1995.)

- In 212 BC, Hannibal gained entrance to and seized the city of Tarentum from the Romans in a deception-produced surprise attack. Hannibal exploited the presence of a dissident Greek resident, Cononeus, to create a nightly ritual: Cononeus departed the city in a large hunting party, ostensibly to gather supplies, and returned in the wee hours, his men laden with game. The Tarentine guards became used to the sight (and grateful for the provender), and greatly relaxed their vigilance. When Hannibal introduced some of his best soldiers into the party, disguised as hunters, the guards barely took notice. Hannibal's men overcame the guards and opened the gates for the body of Hannibal's host, which promptly captured the city with few casualties. (Drawn from Asprey, 1994, and Dunnigan and Nofi, 1995.)

An important point to make here (one visible in the preceding examples) is that deception is rarely an end unto itself. For example, deception is most often used *in coordination with other methods* to create windows of opportunity that expose the enemy (i.e., make him or her vulnerable). Moreover, deception is frequently employed to effect *surprise*, among the most precious commodities in conflict.

WHO WOULD USE DECEPTION?

It is a fundamental contention of this report that deception may be usefully employed by both enemy and friendly forces in the urban environment. Ample historical precedent supports this claim. Deception may target both combatants and noncombatants, and it may do so at all operational levels. This means that deception is a powerful tool in the arsenal of the individual infantryman and the CINC alike.

At the strategic and higher operational levels of war, deception is the purview of the joint force commander's (JFC) cell overseeing, developing, deconflicting, and coordinating all information operations (IO) for the joint force. Deception planning occurs, along with other IO activities, concomitantly with all intelligence and operational activities undertaken by the JFC. Moreover, the tight secrecy and coordination necessary to successfully conduct strategic and operational deception is best obtained by the IO cell fully supported by intelligence activities and "incorporated into the JFC's overall operations planning" (JP 3-13).

At the tactical and lower operational levels of war, deception is conducted in support of the JFC's overall IO objectives and coordinated by the appropriate commander at all levels, including the individual soldier, pilot, etc. The use of deception must be reported to and overseen by every level in the chain of command up to the JFC and the joint command IO cell. This puts the overall IO cell completely "in the know" and ensures that the JFC's objectives are being met and that other deceptions are not compromised or adversely affected by the actions of the unit. The reverse is not true, however, as top-down deception planning preserves secrecy and follows strict "need-to-know" practices.

Consider the following notional examples as a means of sampling the space of possibilities within which deception might be used by a range of actors:

- **An individual sniper moves about the urban battlefield, using camouflage to conceal firing positions.** As with animals, her use of camouflage serves both offensive and defensive purposes. First, she wishes to conceal her presence and position from potential targets such that they are less wary and more exposed to her fire. Second, she wishes to conceal her presence and position from enemy combatants who are seeking to detect and fire upon her. The sniper wishes to create a similar misperception in both targets' minds: namely, that there is no one present in the rubble-strewn street (or whatever background) they're observing.

- **A tank platoon commander orders multispectral close-combat decoys (MCCD) deployed on and around his prepared urban position (at the mouths of alleys, peeking from garages, etc.) in expectation of an enemy encroachment.** The use of such decoys has been demonstrated to significantly enhance the survivability of armored forces; in this case, the use of deception is primarily defensive in nature. His aim is to create in the minds of enemy attackers (whether infantry or armor) fleeting misperceptions (i.e., a tank exists where there is no actual tank). While the longevity of such deception may be measured in seconds or minutes, the value added by its success may prove decisive on the battlefield.

- **A commander with responsibility for the integrated air defenses (IAD) of a major metropolis, faced with an enemy who has greater air power and a doctrine calling for its exploitation, chooses to employ a variety of deceptions to protect and promote his IAD assets.** Deception has both offensive and defensive applications in this case. To protect his forces, the IAD commander may opt to use decoys to absorb air strikes, simulations of damage where none exists, camouflage and concealment of IAD sites, and the like. To make enemy aircraft more vulnerable, he may attempt to condition the enemy pilots to particular patterns of defensive fire, use disinformation to misadvertise the strengths and weaknesses of his IAD, and so forth. The aim of any of these deceptions is to create misperceptions that assist the IAD mission on either offense or defense.

- **An insurgent leader waging an urban campaign of terror opts to employ disinformation and diversions to both degrade enemy command and control and to create a blanket of distracting "noise" to cloak the activities of her operatives.** Deception has both an offensive and a defensive application in this scenario. First, hoaxes and "false-flagging" are used to create numerous misperceptions in the minds of enemy intelligence analysts, rendering their attentions divided and their preparedness degraded. Second, a distracted intelligence service is less likely to find and fix insurgents, increasing their survivability. This brand of ruse may, as one example, take the form of employing local printing presses to generate disinformative pamphlets and posters. A "hoax" pamphlet might advertise a bombing that never occurs, while a "false-flagging" poster may pin the responsibility for an actual bombing on a rival group or an altogether nonexistent entity. Such "noise" worsens enemy preparedness, and thus may better the chance of success in direct action missions, as well as contribute to the surprise when action is undertaken.

- A Joint Task Force Commander (CJTF), charged with conducting a noncombatant evacuation operation (NEO) in a semipermissive urban environment, arranges for false operational plans to be leaked to/intercepted by potential adversaries. These plans, if believed by an opponent determined to thwart the NEO, will have the opponent fortifying the wrong buildings, preparing the wrong avenues, and the like, all at the wrong time and in the wrong way. The goal of this JTF commander is to create a set of misperceptions in the mind of any potential adversary that will serve both defensive and, if necessary, offensive purposes.

- A Joint Force Commander (JFC), commanding U.S. forces in support of a United Nations peacekeeping and nation-building mission, is plagued by guerrilla and terror attacks in built-up areas within his area of responsibility. He employs disinformation, demonstrations, and decoys to root out the infiltrators and insurgents. By creating false targets of opportunity (for example, designating incorrect UN barracks locations in a radio broadcast), phony indicators of vulnerability (e.g., deliberately allowing vehicles too close to false headquarters), and other imaginative falsehoods, the JFC seeks to seize the initiative from the guerrillas/terrorists, divert their attacks to worthless targets, and pierce the veil of anonymity that cloaks their activities. This latter goal is particularly important for an urban setting, with its massive noncombatant population. Deception is used here to create misperceptions about the time, place, units, defensive posture, and other characteristics of potential targets. Deception is thus applied defensively in support of force protection and counterintelligence activities on a large scale within the urban environment. Note that in this case, deception is of necessity targeted at noncombatants deemed to be channels of intelligence for the adversary; this could be the political, social, or cultural leadership.

Deception can be a powerful force multiplier for leaders at all levels of war. As these examples hopefully demonstrate, no side automatically owns a monopoly on the use of deception, and all sides should be prepared to counter it.

HOW IS DECEPTION EMPLOYED?

The Contextual Requirements of Deception

Deception cannot and should not occur in a vacuum. The setting necessary for the conduct of deception can be characterized by the following features. Note that while the phrasing refers to "actors," this is shorthand: it could refer to individual items, such as a tank versus a reconnaissance aircraft, or groups, such as a terrorist cell versus a security agency.

- **Two or more actors are in contention.** This does not necessitate a state of open conflict, only unfriendly rivalry. It is presumed that they are seeking individually advantageous solution(s); this does not necessitate a perfectly zero-sum game, but merely something like it.

- **Information may be acquired, processed, and utilized by all actors: this forms their respective perceptions.** We presume that decisions can be made, and that these decisions are at least shaped in some manner by information about other actors and the environment (i.e., by perceptions). A blind, unthinking actor (or preprogrammed robot) is difficult to deceive.

- **Information may be transmitted between actors.** This may be indirect (i.e., via a third party), but if transmission is impossible then deception is not practicable. This also necessitates the complementarity between the methods of sending and receiving: my false radio transmissions are useless if you are not listening to the radio! Note that any collection of intelligence counts as a transmission of information.

- **The actors operate under conditions of uncertainty (i.e., without complete knowledge).** This is perhaps an epistemological consideration, but important nonetheless. A party that cannot be misled or made unsure cannot be deceived. A party in possession of literally all the pertinent facts, or one thoroughly convinced of the accuracy of its perceptions, is extremely unlikely to be persuaded by contraindicators.

- **The actors possess some flexibility in their courses of action.** While an inflexible target may still be deceived, doing so would be an academic exercise. Deception has utility only if the target takes or refrains from some action that the deceiver can exploit.

It appears that the factors of confusion and high operational tempo, the multiple dimensions of threat and uncertainties, the degradation of intelligence and communications, etc., all of which make urban operations so challenging, create a context (as defined here) eminently suitable to deception. We shall revisit this emerging hypothesis in greater detail in the final chapter of this report.

The Process of Deception

> It is very important to spread rumors among the enemy that you are planning one thing; then go and do something else . . .
>
> —Emperor Maurice, *Strategikon*

Military deceivers have uppermost in mind an *objective:* what it is they want the friendly force to accomplish. This could range from simple survival to gaining strategic surprise. Growing immediately therefrom is a notion of what the deceiver wants the adversary to *do* in order to achieve that objective. This could be as simple as getting the adversary to focus at point A instead of point B at a critical moment, or as complex as inducing the adversary to lower the readiness and preparedness of his nation's defenses over the course of years.

If the deceiver knows what the adversary should do, the next step is to consider *who* can galvanize that action: this person is the *target* of the deception. As noted previously, the target may be a principal in the adversary command structure or an influential noncombatant, for example, a revered religious leader. The deceiver parlays intelligence (HUMINT, SIGINT, etc.) about the target into a profile of that person's preconceptions, beliefs, intentions, and capabilities. A well-constructed deception is built around that intelligence and exploits it. The deceiver answers the question, "What more does the target need to believe in order to incite the actions I desire from him?" This is to say, the deceiver generates a list of misperceptions that must be engendered in the target.

Knowing the beliefs the target must hold to goad him to prejudicial action, the deceiver formulates the *story* that must be told to the target (through a variety of media) to produce those misperceptions. This "story" is told through the means of deception: the classic instruments (such as camouflage or disinformation) that comprise the deceiver's arsenal.

Thus the deception planning process is a "backwards-planning" procedure, which begins with the desired end-state (i.e., the objective) and from that derives the target of the deception, the target's desired response, the requisite misperception, and the "story" that needs to be told. In deception plans, *the ends dictate the means.* This is illustrated in Figure 1.

The actual execution of the deception planning process moves in the reverse direction: informational elements being manipulated are transmitted (or obscured), creating the story, in the mind of the target(s), to achieve the objective. A simple historical example will serve to illustrate the process:

- Facing German submarine warfare prior to World War I, Winston Churchill sought to confuse and entrap German submarines (*the objective*). The entity that controlled German submarines was

RAND *MR1132-1*

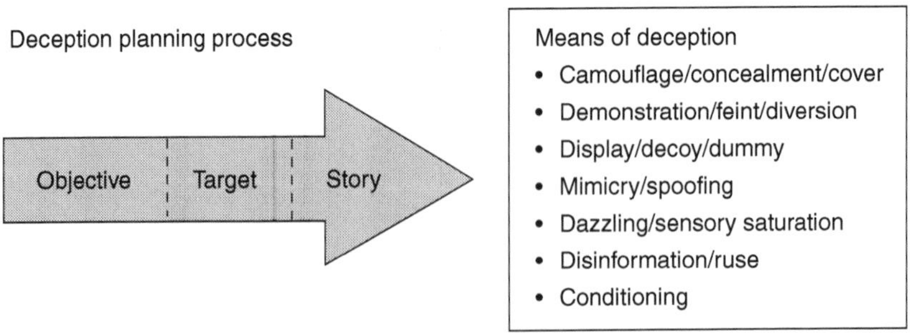

Figure 1—The Deception Planning Process

the German High Seas Fleet (*the target*). Churchill reasoned that the German High Seas Fleet would be baffled and ripe for ambush (*the target response*) if the number and disposition of British vessels were inflated and/or ambiguous (*the misperception*). Churchill therefore urged the construction of numerous decoy, dummy, and notional ships (*the means*) to produce such inflation and/or ambiguity (*the story*).

If we accept the premise previously introduced—that the characteristics of urban operations allow or perhaps facilitate deception—is it any surprise that combatants readying their urban environment for battle will do so to best facilitate the deception process? As noted by Matsulenko (1974, p. 33, emphasis added),

> In October 1942, [Soviet] Engineering Forces prescribed the construction of obstacles, preparation of built-up areas, and delimiting of defensive boundaries *in conjunction* with the development of operational and tactical deception plans.

The Means of Deception

> Let every soldier hew him down a bough, and bear it before him; thereby shall we shadow the numbers of our host, and make discovery err in report of us.
>
> —William Shakespeare, *Macbeth*, Act V, Scene IV

The means of deception are the tools in the deceiver's toolbox. As noted in Joint Pub 3-58: *Joint Doctrine on Military Deception*, they are "[m]ethods, resources, and techniques that can be used to convey information to the deception target."

We note that an imprecision in the definition must be clarified: the term "convey information" can in practice apply to both revealing and concealing data from an adversary. Most deceptions have elements of both, to varying degrees; for example, false radio traffic transmitted along with genuine communications can both cover the genuine signals with obscuring "background noise" and portray a false order of battle to the eavesdropping adversary. In the former, service deception plays a masking role, while in the latter, deception plays a suggestive role.

There are an infinite number of "methods, resources, and techniques" that may be employed in a deception, but they generally group into a finite number of categories. Current joint doctrine generally groups deception into three areas: physical, technical, and administrative (Joint Pub 3-58).

- **Physical means.** Activities and resources used to convey or deny selected information to a foreign power. Examples include military operations (including exercises, reconnaissance, training activities, and movement of forces); the use of dummy equipment and devices; tactics; bases, logistic actions, stockpiles, and repair activity; tests and evaluation activities.

- **Technical means.** Military material resources and their associated operating techniques used to convey or deny selected information to a foreign power through the deliberate radiation, re-radiation, alteration, absorption, or reflection of energy; the emission or suppression of chemical or biological odors; and the emission or suppression of nuclear particles.

- **Administrative means.** Resources, methods, and techniques to convey or deny oral, pictorial, documentary, or other physical evidence to a foreign power.

The above taxonomy focuses upon the form rather than the utility of the means; an alternative would be to focus upon their function:

- **Camouflage/concealment.** The former is the use of natural or artificial material on or about the deceiver to evade detection. The latter is the judicious use of cover and terrain by the deceiver to hide from observation.

- **Demonstration/feint/diversion.** The act of drawing the attention of a target away from an area or activity the deceiver chooses. Demonstrations make no contact with the adversary, while feints do.

- **Display/decoy/dummy.** The placement of a natural or artificial construct away from a deceiver to portray an entity or object of significance to the target.

- **Mimicry/spoofing.** The use of a natural or artificial construct by the deceiver allowing him or her to portray an entity of significance to the target.

- **Dazzling/sensory saturation.** Overloading the sensory processing abilities of the target with an overabundance of stimuli. The principal idea is to raise the "noise" level high enough to drown out the target signal.

- **Disinformation/ruse.** The doctoring of media (printed, electronic, photographic, etc.) passed to the target.

- **Conditioning/exploit.** Either (1) exploiting a target's preexisting bias, belief, or habit, or (2) generating and then exploiting such a bias, belief, or habit. As noted by Collins (1997), "No matter how security-conscious someone is, there is almost always some aspect of his behavior which becomes habitual." Whether the habit is naturally acquired or induced by the would-be deceiver prior to an operation is incidental.

Consider the following example from the January 1995 battle for Grozny:

> [The Chechens] would listen in to Russian units on a captured radio set. When a unit sounded as if they were in trouble and calling for instructions, one of the Chechens would grab the receiver and shout commands in Russian to retreat. (Gall and De Waal, 1998, p. 206.)

Under the current Joint Doctrine definition, this would be considered a *technical* type of deception, conveying erroneous information to adversaries through radiation of false radio signals. Under the second taxonomy scheme, this same deception would be part mimicry and part conditioning/exploit, as functionally the effort is aimed at imitating a trusted source of authority and engendering a preconditioned response.

In practice, deceivers combine material and behavioral elements as needed to craft deceptions based upon operational requirements plus good intelligence of the target. Nearly anything can be drafted into the employ of the deceiver as needed, and the above categories should serve to illustrate the broad range of instruments available. It should also be noted that deception is almost always conducted to further some concurrent activity. Thus, a terrorist might employ a disguise to gain access to a political dignitary's residence. Or a combatant commander might use a diversion to draw enemy forces away from the actual avenue used for an assault. This is not a requirement per se for deception to take place, but deception is seldom seen without it.

HOW USEFUL IS DECEPTION?

It is widely understood that deceptions have aided combatants in both offense and defense for the length of recorded history and the breadth of conflict, from insurgency to invasion. Historical accounts document the employment of deception in a spectrum of environments, supported by a broad range of technologies, both high and low. The following examples, drawn from disparate parts of the spectrum in terms of technology and scale, should serve to suggest that deception is valuable both offensively and defensively, in cities as well as other environments, and in conflicts of varying intensity, regardless of technology and "home turf" advantages.

*   In roughly 1200 BC, Joshua captured the city of Ai by means of deception, shortly after the fall of Jericho. After suffering a minor defeat in his first attempt at taking the city, Joshua devised a ruse that has been repeated countless times since: the feigned retreat. Arraying the bulk of his host before the gates of Ai, Joshua offered battle, all the while hiding a goodly portion of his force to the rear of the city, out of sight. When the soldiers of Ai took the field and began battling his men, Joshua ordered a retreat designed to look as if it were a rout. When the exultant men of Ai came after them, Joshua's hidden force emerged and stormed Ai, overwhelming the skeletal force left behind and seizing the city. As the news hit the men of Ai their charge faltered, and Joshua wheeled his force and pinned them between his men and the now-captured city. Their force in disarray, the men of Ai were slaughtered. (Drawn from Handel, 1985, and Dunnigan and Nofi, 1995.)

*   In September of 1864, the Confederate guerrilla fighter Nathan Bedford Forrest surrounded a well-defended Union fort at Athens, Alabama. Forrest's force numbered about 4,500, while the dug-in Union force at the fort numbered under 2,000. Forrest suspected the unpleasant outcome of any attack against a

prepared, well-armed enemy in built-up terrain, and further knew that reinforcements were on their way to relieve the beleaguered Union defenders. Forrest arranged a parley with the fort's commander, Colonel Wallace Campbell, and contrived an artful deception to receive him. In a trick that Erwin Rommel would repeat in Tripoli nearly a hundred years later, Forrest arranged for Campbell to be given a tour of the besieging force— all the while having each unit that Campbell left pack up and be placed in his path again. This clever bit of trickery convinced Campbell that he faced a force roughly four times his own and induced him to promptly surrender without a fight. (Drawn from Asprey, 1994, and Dunnigan and Nofi, 1995.)

- The Battle of Kursk, in mid-1943, demonstrated the powerful— indeed decisive—leverage deception offered to combatants on both the offense and defense at the strategic and operational levels. The Germans massed an enormous combined force in their offensive against the Soviet Union at the Kursk "Bulge." A worried Soviet High Command (STAVKA) generated strategic and operational defense plans thoroughly incorporating *maskirovka* [deception and OPSEC] measures. Moreover, *maskirovka* was employed to conceal preparations for Soviet offensives to follow hard upon the heels of the defense. The deception measures included diversionary operations (feints and demonstrations), false troop and logistics concentrations, false and confusing radio traffic, false airfields and aircraft, and the dissemination of false rumors both at the front and in German-held areas. (Drawn from Glantz, 1989.)

- The successful terrorist/revolutionary 1946–1948 campaign of the Zionists to drive the British from Palestine in the aftermath of World War II and establish a Jewish state has, as its pivotal event, the perpetration of a deception. The Irgun, led by Menachem Begin, used a well-crafted and precisely targeted deception to erode British mettle and energize the Irgun's popular support. British forces, who had annually suppressed Yom Kippur [Day of Atonement] rites at the Western Wall, were fed false (but persuasive) information by the Irgun that the upcoming event would be attended by Irgun members in force, who were prepared to violently resist any British suppression. The methods included English-language pamphlets and rumors circulated through informers. In reality, no Irgun members were to attend (although no one but the Irgun would know this). The British backed away from the supposed confrontation, and this policy change was trumpeted by the Irgun as a major victory for themselves and for all Jews. (Drawn from Begin, 1972.)

- In 1990–1991, "DESERT STORM demonstrated the effectiveness of the integrated use of operational security (OPSEC) and deception to shape the beliefs of the adversary commander and achieve surprise. Deception and OPSEC efforts were combined to convince Saddam Hussein of a Coalition intent to conduct the main offensive using ground and amphibious attacks into central Kuwait, and to dismiss real indicators of the true Coalition intent to swing west of the Iraqi defenses in Kuwait and make the main attack into Iraq itself . . . Deception measures included broadcasting tank noises over loudspeakers and deploying dummy tanks and artillery pieces as well as simulated HQ radio traffic to fake the electronic signatures of old unit locations." (*Joint Staff Special Technical Operations Division*, quoted in JP 3-13.)

If history is any guide, deception (particularly in coordination with other IO methods) can be a valuable force multiplier at any of the levels of war or peace, in crisis or in conflict.

WHAT ARE THE DANGERS OF EMPLOYING DECEPTION?

> Oh, what a tangled web we weave, when first we practice to deceive!
>
> —Sir Walter Scott, *Marmion*

Deception is admittedly a double-edged sword: lethal when wielded competently, dangerous if mishandled. As noted in JP 3-58, "deception planners must carefully consider the risks versus the possible benefits of the deception." There are three fundamental challenges to the employment of deception: cost, deconfliction, and discovery.

As noted in current doctrine (JP 3-13), practicing deception successfully may be among the most rewarding of investments but it also requires an expense:

Military deception operations are a powerful tool in full-dimensional operations, but are not without cost. Forces and resources must be committed to the deception effort to make it believable, possibly to the short-term detriment of some aspects of the campaign or operation.

It is also critical that deception is properly coordinated and overseen so as not to create confusion or fratricide among friendly forces. For example, a camouflaged soldier lying in wait wants to ensure that while he is undetected by the enemy, his location and identification are known to friendly forces, for obvious reasons. At a higher operational level, a combatant commander who employs false radio transmissions to dupe the enemy into thinking his forces will be imminently attacking an enemy-held town in force must be careful to ensure that such a deception does not drive noncombatants living in the town into a panicked and dangerous flight. The processes of carefully screening and targeting deceptive efforts to affect only the desired target are known collectively as deconfliction.

In the dynamic environment of a military operation, it is imperative that deception planners carefully and continually monitor (and reexamine as necessary) all the components of the deception process: objective, target, story, and means. One key reason for this is the need to be able to mitigate damage should the deception be discovered. As noted in joint doctrine concerning deception (JP 3-58), deceivers must be wary of "deception failure, exposure of means or feedback channels, and unintended effects." The danger of deception exposed can be grave, as was the case when the British exposed and turned every German spy in England during World War II. This provided the British with an excellent tool for perpetrating their own schemes against the Germans.

Finally, a consideration of the legality of employing deception is warranted. Deception is in principle coordinated with command and control warfare (C2W), civil affairs, psychological operations, and public affairs to harmoniously advance U.S. military interests. In practice, however, the generation and dissemination of patently false or misleading information is a complex, evolving, and legally murky issue. As noted in Joint Publication 3-58, it is generally accepted that U.S. forces may employ deception (whether administrative, physical, or technical) against hostile forces with impunity (in a legal or ethical sense). Further, it is contrary to U.S. policy to deliberately misinform or mislead the U.S. public or U.S. decisionmakers (leaving room for operational security/secrecy). However, in between these two poles is a great, gray area that may have a significant impact on military outcomes. What about employing deception against neutral or un-friendly forces not directly involved in the operation? Against non-combatants (particularly influential ones) friendly to an adversary? Against NGOs? What if deceptive information targeted against an adversary leaks out to international news media and is then fed back to the American public? The answers to these questions are unclear, which traditionally means that if the stakes are high, then all is permitted that is not expressly forbidden. While a thorough treat-ment of this topic is beyond the scope of this report, the interested reader may find a useful and up-to-date discussion in Greenberg, Goodman, and Soo Hoo (1999).

Chapter Four

THE ROLE OF DECEPTION IN URBAN OPERATIONS

To achieve victory we must as far as possible make the enemy blind and deaf by sealing his eyes and ears, and drive his commanders to distraction by creating confusion in their minds.

—Mao Tse-tung, *On Protracted War*

The following four propositions, culled from the "Modern Maxims for Urban Warfare" in Marine Corps Warfighting Publication 3-35.3, suggest the powerful influence that deception may have upon urban outcomes:

- **Intelligence is imperative to success in urban warfare.** As discussed previously, the paramount aim of deception is to provide the adversary with poor intelligence (misperceptions), worsening his decisionmaking (decisionmaking being the overall target of IO generally). Note that we treat the term "intelligence" interchangeably with "perception," in the sense that both are a product of the information collected plus the processing done. Intelligence is vital at all levels of war: the squad leader needs to be advised of rifle fire coming from a nearby building; the joint force commander needs overhead imagery indicating the creation of obstacle belts by hostile forces; and the NCA need to know the factional infighting in the enemy command structure.

- **Surprise attack can substantially reduce the cost of attacking an urban area.** Analytical support for this tenet has been provided by Whaley (1969), who estimated that surprise changed the ratio of casualties in favor of an attacker from 1:1 to 5:1. It is important to note that surprise is an *effect* with many possible *causes*:

deception is but one. Technological or doctrinal innovations, tight secrecy, and a sluggish adversary can also beget surprise. However, deception is increasingly the surest effector of surprise. In Barton Whaley's magnum opus *Stratagem* (1969), he notes that in 68 major battles between 1914 and 1967, the incidence of surprise (where present) became steadily more reliant upon deception.

- **Surprise is a combat multiplier for both the attacker and defender.** Virtually every military theorist, from Frontinus to Liddell-Hart, would agree with this proposition. Analytical support for it is provided by DePuy (1978), who estimated that the element of surprise doubled the combat power of those who had it. Betts (1983) has made similar points, relating to the induction of paralysis when surprise is effected. Deception has emerged as the preeminent "midwife of surprise" (Harris, 1970) at the end of the 20th century, and thus it plays a vital role in any doctrine calling for surprise.

- **Media coverage of urban warfare can have operational or strategic impact.** The propagation of deception to the intended target via news and other media has a long and storied past. However, the use of deception to influence and manage the media has also proved to be a valuable objective.

It seems clear that current doctrine on urban operations not only allows for, but indeed actively prescribes, measures that may worsen enemy decisionmaking, leave an enemy ripe for surprise, and influence media coverage in a manner favorable to friendly forces. Deception ably fits the job description.

WHAT KIND OF URBAN OPERATIONS IS DECEPTION APPLICABLE TO?

It would be an exaggeration to say that successful deception by itself enables wars to be won. But it is precisely when the resources are stretched and the tasks many, when the forces are evenly matched and the issue trembles in the balance, that successful deception matters most.

—David Dilks, *Appeasement and Intelligence*,
quoted by Handel (1985)

Deception is a powerful instrument for virtually every type of urban operation, since to succeed nearly every one will require accurate intelligence, friendly (or at least neutral) news coverage, and perhaps surprise—in short, wherever the four Marine Corps maxims we quoted earlier may apply. However, we are cognizant that the mission undertaken, the stakes involved, and the facts on the ground may not allow "every trick in the book" to be used. This is particularly true if cost, deconfliction, and discovery concerns are nontrivial.

For the weaker of two contenders, or for the side that has prior possession of the built-up area in question, deception pays potentially huge dividends for acceptable investments. This premise is relatively easy to accept given the earlier points about why a weaker combatant might seek to invite battle in urban terrain (if the urban environment increases one's own combat power or decreases an opponent's). Deception is similarly inviting: if deception can yield surprise, and surprise can significantly increase combat power, then the weaker side is likely to resort to deception. As proposed earlier, these independent asymmetric strategies may have cumulative or even synergistic effects.

However, deception need not be remanded to the exclusive custody of David. Returning to the earlier example, imagine how differently the parable might have turned out had Goliath employed wit in addition to brawn. It may prove an illustrative exercise to construct a notional example of an urban operation with friendly forces projecting force, wherein deception is employed. This may better clarify the interrelationship between the deception and urban terrain, particularly insofar as Goliath might be concerned.

Scenario: A U.S. joint task force is assigned the responsibility for the noncombatant evacuation operation (NEO) of several hundred Americans in a large port city within a nonaligned developing nation. The *casus belli* for the NEO is a breakdown in civic order and the eruption of factional strife in the city and its environs. The setting for the NEO is thus labeled semipermissive, with both organized and impromptu resistance expected, probably in the form of ambushes and raids featuring small arms and RPG fire. International organizations (including relief agencies and news media) are present, along with just shy of a million panicky noncombatants caught in the crossfire. Thus restrictive rules of engagement (ROE) are in place to avoid excessive noncombatant casualties and any other impolitic events. Traditional "clear and hold" sector-by-sector methods are inapplicable as an overall approach, given the size of the friendly force and the size of the built-up area. A speedy, penetrating thrust to the American citizens' rallying point (an embassy, hotel, or the like) causing minimal collateral damage, yet ensuring the safety of the force, is a better bet.

- *What would deception be used for?* Deception could be used to help achieve operational objectives: effecting surprise for friendly forces, drawing hostile forces away from rally points, turning hostile forces out of prepared positions, and the like. Tactical objectives can also be gained with the help of deception: concealing an axis of advance from hostile intelligence, catching hostage-takers off guard, drawing enemy fire away from friendly forces, and so on. Put another way, deception would be employed consonantly with IO objectives generally, and the Marine Corps maxims noted above specifically: that is, feeding the adversary poor intelligence, achieving operational and tactical surprise, and influencing the news media in a manner favorable to strategic and operational objectives.

- *Who would use deception?* The friendly JTF commander and his or her staff could certainly make use of deception to help achieve operational objectives enumerated above. Smaller unit leaders and even individual soldiers could similarly make use of deception, in their case to achieve tactical objectives.

- *Is the context necessary for deception present?* Reviewing the criteria listed in Chapter Three, pp. 26–27, the JTF commander plus his staff can definitely answer this question. Close coordination with friendly intelligence is critical in this assessment, underlining the directives found in Joint Pubs 3-13 and 3-58. In this case there are at least two sides in contention (friendly plus one or more adversaries plus noncombatants), *and* the adversaries and noncombatants are gathering information about the evolving situation, *and* the friendly force has the means at its disposal for transmitting information to the adversaries and noncombatants, *and* the adversaries and noncombatants won't automatically "see right through" any falsehoods, *and* the adversaries and noncombatants can actually modify their actions based upon information gathered. Deception may be gainfully employed in this scenario, given that concerns over cost, deconfliction, and discovery are not too great. While these criteria may sound stringent, in practice it is most often the case that they are fulfilled at one or more levels of war.

- *Can the process and means of deception be employed?* At the operational level, with the objectives for any deceptions noted above, the JTF commander plus his staff must decide whether accessible decisionmakers (adversaries or neutrals) can be targeted and swayed by deception operations. If such targets exist, they ask, can the appropriate story be concocted, delivered, and digested by the target in a way that will engender useful and timely responses? If the answer to the preceding questions is yes, then deception surely offers itself as an important measure to assist the NEO.

The example of the NEO is a useful one. It represents an emerging class of missions likely to be performed by U.S. forces, either alone or in concert; moreover, it is a simple exercise to extrapolate how the use of deception seen in this case might be applicable to smaller-scale contingencies as well as the higher end of the conflict spectrum. In sum, in any urban operation wherein enemy intelligence, media coverage, and surprise (with all its benefits) play a role, deception can perform an important function.

HOW DOES URBAN TERRAIN ALTER DECEPTION?

> IRA volunteers operating in rural areas, wanting to blend in with the hedges, fields and trees, could wear such jackets, *but they were not the gear for towns and villages.* You had to blend in with the local *population:* you had to look like a mechanic, or a postman, or a bank clerk, not Fidel Castro.
>
> —Collins (1997, p. 171, emphasis added)

In a previous section we noted several key differences between urban and other types of terrain. Likewise, deception methods and means vary between environments. It is a straightforward proposition, based upon our earlier discussion of the contextual requirements and process, that effective deceptions must be tailored to suit their context. In a rudimentary illustration of this principle, it stands to reason that camouflage useful in woodland settings is of little use in the midst of a steel-and-stone metropolis. The particular character-istics of the urban environment have a direct influence upon the implementation of deception methods, whether camouflage or decoy, diversion or disinformation. While little experimentation has been done to map the parameters of this phenomenon in military applications, some work has been done along these lines in animals (Erichsen, Krebs, and Houston, 1980).

The case of camouflage in urban terrain is an interesting representa-tive of deception more generally. Current Marine Corps doctrine (MCWP 3-35.3) is clear:

> To survive and win in combat in built-up areas, a unit should sup-plement cover and concealment with camouflage. To properly camouflage men, carriers, and equipment, Marines should study the surrounding area and make their fighting positions blend with the local terrain.

What does this admonishment translate to in practice? What are the specific features of urban terrain relevant to camouflage? As noted in Schecter and Farrar (1983), "the texture of urban terrain is very abrupt, truncating line-of-sight envelopes severely from most loca-tions," meaning close detection ranges are the norm. Structures in built-up areas throw sharp shadows that shift during the day. Stone, brick, and masonry predominate, yet intermittent bursts of color are common: the particulars matter greatly and can vary from block to block. Soft, organic curves are far less frequent in urban terrain than in any other. Light penetrates poorly into the interiors of buildings. Smog, soot, dust, and haze are regular features of most urban cityscapes, and in conflict this is worsened by the presence of smoke.

Therefore, camouflage in urban terrain—*if it is to be useful*—must account for all of these factors. It must be effective at the short ranges frequent in urban encounters, in shadows and broad daylight, in open air or choking dust, and against the singular color schemes of the cityscape. As noted by the U.S. Army Soldier Systems Center at Natick, Massachusetts, camouflage in urban terrain requires

smaller designs with closer merge distances. Also, urban back-
grounds generally require more straight edge camouflage, vertical
and horizontal designs to blend with homes, buildings and other
urban structures, etc. Near infrared (NIR) camouflage for urban
areas would generally mimic NIR spectral reflectance of road and
building materials, asphalt, concrete, gravel, steel, brick, wood,
stucco, etc. This would be in contrast to woodland NIR requirements that mimic the chlorophyll [spectral reflectance] curve of
vegetation, and the NIR requirements of desert camouflage which
mimics the [spectral reflectance] curves of desert sands.

Other forms of deception are similarly influenced by their context,
particularly by the key characteristics of urban terrain noted earlier.
Generally speaking, deception is not only *altered* (as noted above),
but significantly *abetted* when conducted on urban terrain.

HOW DOES URBAN TERRAIN HELP DECEPTION?

[S]etting traps: places where the [police] were always pulling raids. One
of our girls would call them up and say "Listen, there's been a burglary
at a drug store. Why don't you send a radio car over?" And then these
two radio cars would come by and everyone would be standing by the
corner with rocks and molotovs, and then: bang!

—Baumann (1975, p. 52)

Hypotheses on Deception in Urban Operations

Judging from the characteristics of urban terrain, their effects upon
operations, and the nature of deception, it appears that urban terrain
amplifies the ease and effectiveness of deception in six key ways:

The scope of deception is increased. The size and complexity of
deception efforts in built-up areas is fundamentally increased. The
axiom that urban terrain swallows units with an appetite unmatched
by any other environment has a flip side: urban terrain can accom-
modate very large numbers of men and materiel. Recall the com-
ment noted earlier by Ellefsen (1987) with regard to the multiplica-
tion of surface space within a city. The net effect of this is to greatly
expand the physical and logical reaches of deception efforts in urban
geography. For example, it may be possible to camouflage or con-

ceal the presence of three companies of dismounts in an urban area, whereas only a single company might be concealed in a similar-sized area of desert. Similar questions arise with regard to vehicles and command posts: how much more can be concentrated and covered in an urban environment than in other environments? The Soviets recognized this principle in World War II, as noted by Matsulenko (1974):

> The city environment allowed for effective concealment and camouflage of massive concentrating forces . . . better than any other operating environments.

No experimental data currently exist to quantify these phenomena, except in animal biology. As an interesting aside, the question of what effect the urban environment has on operational security, deconfliction, and logistical efforts also remains unanswered.

"Background noise" provides an excellent framework for deception efforts. Confusion and complexity make intelligence efforts more difficult in general; deception exploits these features when possible. As Roberta Wohlstetter proposed in her analysis of Pearl Harbor (1962), skillful deception can capitalize upon inherent ambiguity and volume of indicators, "heightening the impression that evidence is indeterminate." No operating environment is "noisier" than the city, with its surfeit of structures, avenues, radio and telephonic traffic, noncombatant vehicles and pedestrians, noise, and heat. Not only is it difficult to discern militarily important "signals" from the ambient "noise," but a wily adversary will *deliberately* foster more such clamor and cloak his activities and intentions behind that backdrop. But in addition to enhancing concealment, there may be some interesting effects in the other direction as well. To recall an earlier example, the crying wolf ploy is an active attempt to reduce an adversary's readiness and vigilance through repetitive, visible "exercises." Is crying wolf easier or harder to accomplish in an urban environment than in others? Are intelligence analysts who scrutinize the city more or less prone to be searching for preconceived patterns than those looking at other environments? Once again, no experimental data exist to quantify how urbanized terrain affects the concealing *or* revealing of deceptions in built-up areas.

The city is a rich source of material resources for deception. Deception requires varying degrees of investment, and investment requires resources. While some combatants may have the requisite materials in their own inventory, others will have to exploit some aspect of the local environment. Built-up areas (particularly cities) provide a lode of material wealth not found in any other environment: communications and energy infrastructure, manufacturing facilities and fabric, vehicles and scrap, printing and xerographic facilities, paints, fuels, weapons and explosives, and of course, noncombatants and organizations of every stripe. Whether the deception method in question is camouflage, decoy, diversion, disinformation, or something else, the physical and contextual requirements to carry it off are more likely to be present in urban terrain than in any other. A superb example of this is recounted by Roy Stanley (1998, p. 171), describing the masterwork of camouflage undertaken in 1942 to protect the Douglas Aircraft Company factory in Santa Monica, California, from the threat of Japanese bombing:

> A key factor in this story was the special pool of talent available in Hollywood, all eager to help the war effort. Movie studios were full of experts in creating illusion and they had the tools, experience, skills and enthusiasm. They understood how to use wood, wire, plaster and paint to shape or reshape something.

The Germans took similar advantage of Italian movie studios in creating deceptions at Anzio. While certainly not all built-up areas will have local Hollywoods, they will all have reservoirs of men and materiel in the noncombatant population and infrastructure unavailable to combatants in any other type of terrain. This could be as simple (but powerful) as Xerox machines and department store mannequins, from which a hundred clever deceptions might be wrought.

Decisionmaking is hastier and generally less informed in built-up areas. As clearly indicated in JP 3-13, *Joint Doctrine for Information Operations,* worsening an opponent's decision-making process is a powerful enhancement to operations—and the stated goal of all offensive IO measures (including deception). As noted earlier, urban operations feature degraded command and control (C2), great stress, and a high operational tempo. In other words, combatants' decisionmaking is adversely affected *just by participating* in urban operations. Specifically, a high operational tempo necessitates that unit leaders make faster decisions, and degraded C2 implies that the intelligence picture remains incomplete during those decisions. This is fertile ground for deceivers. Consider, as noted in the contextual requirements for deception, that a less-informed adversary is more gullible. Consider also the Marine Corps maxim calling for intelligence as an essential component to success in urban operations. Deception injects false indicators into an already poorly "intelligenced" environment. For example, given the importance of navigation and orientation in the complex urban environment, maps make an excellent subject of disinformation campaigns:

> In the 1930s, after the NKVD, or security police, assumed control of mapmaking, the Soviet cartographic bureaucracy began to deliberately distort the position and form of villages, coastlines, rivers, highways, railroads, buildings, boundaries and other features shown on maps and atlases for public use. (Monmonier, 1996, p. 115.)

In a fast-paced urban operation, the need for speedy decisions worsens a target's ability to discount false indicators (Schul, Burnstein, and Bardi, 1996; Fein and Hilton, 1994). Moreover, less-informed individuals are generally less able to penetrate deceptions than more-informed individuals (Anderson, Lepper, and Ross, 1980).

The presence of noncombatants significantly worsens the capability of discerning friend from foe, and combatant from noncombatant. The presence of noncombatants in great numbers and great variety creates significant challenges for forces in urban operations. One such challenge is the generation of "background noise" mentioned above, but another is in greatly increasing the difficulty of establishing who's who on the battlefield. This observation is confirmed by West German terrorist Michael Baumann (1975, p. 54):

> The Berlin police were looking for hundreds of groups and sects . . . when all along it was the same crew, who adopted a new name every week.

Rules of engagement (ROE) generally require that noncombatants remain unmolested, and thus it is incumbent upon U.S. forces to establish identity before engaging any target. Noncombatants appear on the urban battlefield with greater frequency and in greater numbers than in any other environment, and thus the burden upon U.S. forces to establish identity is heavier. Not every detection is an enemy to be fired upon, and the diversity of a city's population creates ample opportunities for adversaries to disguise themselves. Moreover, knowing that U.S. forces will be reluctant to fire upon noncombatants, adversaries are likely to deliberately mix with civilian populations to camouflage their presence. This is true in any case, but it is a particularly vexing problem for the side to whom the noncombatant population is unfriendly. An excellent example of this is illustrated by Christmas (1977, p. 23) in his description of the Marines fighting in Hue City, 1968:

> [T]he company had been warned that Viet Cong units occupied the hospital and might pose as patients. They did! In fact, more than one Marine was fired on by "patients," but they were ready for such surprises. A Marine encountered a person wearing a black habit whom he believed to be a nun. He could not have been more wrong. Fortunately the nun's pistol misfired and the Marine's life was spared. The nun was a Viet Cong soldier.

Ruthless adversaries are also likely to employ noncombatants as living decoys and diversions, further complicating the picture for U.S. forces. These techniques have great offensive *and* defensive value, allowing adversaries to materialize close to friendly forces with alarming speed, and to disappear just as quickly into the teeming city. Consider the following example (drawn from a 1991 attack on the British Prime Minister by the IRA):

> The Mark 10 mortar, cunningly constructed from three oxyacetylene cylinders and arranged on a rack with rubber collars at their base to cushion the recoil, could be hidden in a van. The propellant, made from sugar and sodium chlorate, would send the projectiles, each packed with forty pounds of industrial explosive, in a predetermined arc ... To the innocent eye the [nondescript] van would not even seem to be near the heavily protected buildings two hundred yards away ... So on the morning of February 7, 1991, with the roof cut open, with the mortars ready, with the timer fuse ready, the van was driven through an unexpected snow to a site two hundred yards away from Downing Street [the British Prime Minister's residence]. The driver parked, got out into the snow, walked a

few steps and jumped on the [rear seat] of a waiting motorcycle. The short timer was running. (Bell, 1997, pp. 623–624.)

Note how deceptive elements and features of urban terrain so easily intermix. Could a mortar be easily driven to within 200 yards of a country's leadership in any other kind of terrain? Could the weapon be leisurely armed and left to fire without causing even a raised eyebrow, unless it was concealed in an unassuming van? Could the attackers so easily and quickly escape in any other kind of environment?

Urban clutter blunts the edge of technology, particularly with regard to sensors and communications. Technological preeminence is exploited to the hilt in current and future U.S. doctrine. The technological disparity between U.S. forces and potential adversaries—and the resulting advantages accrued—varies with the terrain. Jungles tighten the gap while deserts widen it, but nowhere is the margin slimmer than in built-up areas. Sensors and communications operate less reliably and at reduced power in urban terrain. This fundamentally affects deception by reducing the number and power of intelligence channels available to the target. Of IMINT, SIGINT, HUMINT, COMINT, and MASINT, one or more may be indeterminate, occluded, or untrustworthy. Parenthetically, HUMINT sources may in fact be multiplied greatly in the urban environment, although the trustworthiness and quality of those sources is not at all assured. That said, multiple channels of corroborating intelligence are vital to the penetration of deception. If these intelligence channels are less reliable or absent altogether, vulnerability to deception is increased.

The net result of these six effects is twofold. First, while deception is widely understood to be a powerful tool under many circumstances, *it is particularly effective in the urban environment*, and can be gainfully employed by either side. Second, the weaker of any combatants will assuredly seek to make use of deception, particularly if they are in prior possession of the built-up area, and/or have a friendly relationship with the noncombatant population. This latter assertion is concordant with the tenets of an "asymmetric approach" described earlier.

Historical Support for Hypotheses

> The most powerful weapon of war is the unexpected.
>
> —Julius Caesar, *Commentarii de Bello Gallico*

There is ample historical evidence for the potent admixture of deception plus the urban environment, although there is virtually no experimental data to attempt to measure the impact. Detailed historical case studies are beyond the scope of this report, but a brief look at some recent urban campaigns will prove illustrative. Table 2 introduces this section with a cursory tabulation and comparison of the role of deception in three such urban campaigns.

Battle for Grozny In Chechnya, Russia: January 1995. In late 1994, Russian forces mobilized to stem the separatist tide in the republic of Chechnya. Throughout the month of January 1995, Russian forces fought insurgent Chechens in the streets of the capital city Grozny in a bloody and difficult battle that could fairly be characterized as an unmitigated disaster for Russian forces on their own soil (Thomas, 1997; Lieven, 1998; Gall and De Waal, 1998). The already great challenges of operating in urban terrain against an implacable insurgent force were heightened by Russian failures to train and organize properly, to ensure good intelligence collection and dissemination, to implement good command and control (C2), and to influence the media favorably. The preceding list eerily echoes the discussion earlier of areas that may be exploited by deception methods: the Chechens made good use of these vulnerabilities. From the start, they baited the more-powerful Russian force with an appearance of weakness:

> To all appearances, the Chechen preparations were [worthless], their mission suicidal. As the Russian tanks ranged across the hills to the north of Grozny, attacking a line of villages . . . the Chechens appeared to be doing little to prepare defenses. (Gall and De Waal, 1998, p. 189.)

Table 2

A Look at Hypotheses in Selected Urban Conflicts

	Grozny 1995	Lima, 1985–1989	Belfast/Derry, 1969–1989
Increased scope of deceptions	MTW; thousands of Chechen fighters exploiting deception successfully to confuse and entrap Russians and to force-protect	Terror campaign; hundreds of Sendero Luminoso (SL) operatives organize, recruit, train, plan, and strike in Lima aided by deception	Long-lived terror campaign; hundreds of IRA Provos bomb, snipe, infil/exfil, organize, and persist aided by deception
High-volume background noise	MTW; city in complete chaos	Tumult of a major metropolis with massive slums; discord deliberately intensified by SL	Profusion of targets (across UK) and decentralized nature of IRA create difficulties for British
Increased resources available in urban environment	News media; civilian commo; printing presses; weapons, vehicles; clothes; fuel; HUMINT; etc.	Vehicles; clothes; fuel; printing presses; weapons, HUMINT; etc.	Money; weapons; vehicles; clothes; fuel; news media; civilian commo; printing presses; Catholic safehouses; HUMINT; etc.
Worsened decision-making	Poor Russian C2; Russians surprised	Peruvian intelligence forced to double and redouble assets to cope with deception	British learn from early failures and difficulties, yet persistent utility of deception for IRA
Great numbers of noncombatants present	Tens of thousands unfriendly to Russian troops; ROE attempted; NGOs present	Hundreds of thousands of poor and alienated peasants in slums	Noncombatants are both geographically as well as ideologically divided; ROE for British
Technological edges blunted	Commo degraded; intel sensors degraded; armor vulnerable; weapons less effective; etc.	Not as serious a problem for government as "background noise" issue	Measure versus countermeasure race established; an exception: night vision for British always useful

Chechens employed deception at both the strategic and tactical levels of war with great effect (Thomas, 1997; Lieven, 1998). At the tactical level, Chechen fighters and Ukrainian mercenaries disguised themselves and their vehicles as Russian or noncombatant (including Red Cross); commingled forces with noncombatant crowds and activities when moving in advance or retreat; camouflaged firing points, command posts, and other important sites; employed decoys and dummies to draw fire or confuse Russian intelligence; and transmitted false radio broadcasts to misdirect and disorient Russian troops. At the strategic level, the Chechens assiduously courted the media with a disinformation campaign to present a prejudicial view of the situation; disguised and dispersed forces in and out of theater for intelligence-gathering forays; and targeted neighboring republics' civil and military leaders with disinformation to attempt to widen the war and pin down Russian troops elsewhere. Sergei Stepashin, then head of Russian domestic intelligence (the FSK) and former Russian Prime Minister, made this sardonic observation at the time:

> Yes, the Russian administration has lost the information war. How brilliantly the Chechnyan Minister of Information Movladi Udugov works, how artfully and easily he releases to the press any distortion, lie, juggling of the facts . . . (Quoted in Lieven, 1998, p. 120.)

While the Russians too employed deceptive techniques during the battle for Grozny, sometimes effectively, the Chechens appear to have truly multiplied their combat power by its use. The Russians failed to meet the operational challenges presented by urban terrain and, moreover, failed to ameliorate the specific vulnerabilities to deception noted earlier. This vulnerability to deception efforts (and the Chechen exploitation of it) is responsible, at least in part, for the catastrophic defeat suffered by the Russians in the battle of Grozny.

Urban Campaign of the Sendero Luminoso in Lima, Peru: 1985–1989. Urban terrorism and guerrilla action has a long and venerable tradition in Latin America, playing key roles in Uruguayan (1965–1973), Brazilian (1968–1970), and Argentinean (1970–1976) insurgencies (Marighella, 1968; Jenkins, 1971; Miller, 1980). Urban actions also contributed to Cuban, Guatemalan, and Venezuelan insurgencies between 1957 and 1974 (O'Neill, Heaton, and Alberts, 1980). A more recent and particularly tenacious urban campaign has been waged by the Sendero Luminoso (SL), a devoutly Maoist-Leninist revolutionary group in Peru (McCormick, 1990, 1992). SL (which is still active, though weakened by the decapitation of the organization) has engaged in activities ranging from bombings and assassinations to mobilizing massive demonstrations and propaganda releases in the course of their urban efforts. To operate and be effective in Lima, the capital and heart of the country, SL has employed numerous forms of deception at all levels of war (McCormick, 1990, 1992; Centro de Estudios y Promoción del Desarollo). To achieve its tactical objectives, SL has employed camouflaged sniping positions, disguises and forged identities, diversionary explosions, and the like. At the strategic level, SL has deliberately sought to cloak its activities in the noisy environment of the city, and even to intensify that "background noise" to further befuddle Peruvian intelligence (Sendero Luminoso Documents, 1982, 1987, 1988; Guzman, 1988). This strategy is concordant with the teachings of Carlos Marighella (1968), the premier theoretician of urban guerrilla warfare in the 1960s and 1970s:

> By making expropriations seem the work of bandits and by avoiding identifying themselves and their origins, the Brazilian revolutionaries managed to gain time by keeping the authorities in a state of uncertainty, preventing them from following specific trails.

The unique characteristics of the city, its slums and teeming population, its news media and physical resources, its profusion of activity and traffic—all have served the SL's purposes in promoting its actions and shielding its operatives from detection and neutralization.

Urban Campaign of the Provisional IRA in Belfast/Londonderry: 1969–1989. Since 1916, Irish Republicans determined to gain independence from the British have waged an episodic, evolving campaign for a self-governing, predominately Catholic Northern Ireland. Beginning in 1969–1970 with the formation of the Provisional wing of the IRA, the Republicans brought their efforts to urban centers such as Belfast and Londonderry in earnest. As described by Bell (1997, p. 378), the aggressive British responses to these urban efforts encouraged the IRA to move from a defensive to an offensive campaign. By employing against the IRA the "appropriate" tactics to counter an urban guerrilla campaign, the British Army largely transformed the rocks and riots of 1969 and 1970 into a very real, if low-intensity, war the following year, with snipers, car-bombs, shootouts in housing estates, and battles on the border.

With the intensification of the urban conflict, IRA strategies began to employ deception efforts in a widespread way (Bell, 1991; Dewar, 1992). Deception was employed tactically to assist in the execution of direct action missions: IRA operatives employed disguises and proxies for intelligence gathering and infiltration/exfiltration of active service units (ASU) (Collins, 1997); and diversionary activities (explosions, shots, etc.) were used to draw British/Loyalist forces both away from IRA operatives *and* toward ambushes.

In an example of deception employed at the strategic level, Provisionals fed disinformation (by pamphlet, doctored photo, radio broadcast, etc.) to religious, cultural, civic, and military leaders in order to alienate the British and Loyalists from the noncombatant population (Collins, 1997).

At the operational level, IRA activities were also organized somewhat to foment urban "background noise" when and where needed, as well as to establish patterns of activity to be perceived by British forces. This latter bit of artifice was attempted because the Republicans could exploit the time element of their urban campaign: as noted in the discussion of deception earlier, patterns may be established only to be broken at a choice moment, often to gain tactical or operational surprise (Axelrod, 1979). An extended length of time was not the only factor to be capitalized upon by the IRA. The Provisionals benefited substantially from the presence of a friendly noncombatant population (predominately Catholic) in enclaves, who were alienated from the British. Some Catholic areas became virtually no-go to British forces. Moreover, in the early phases of the urban campaign, IRA forces tactically exploited weaknesses in British command and control, lack of intelligence, and alienation from the population to great effect. As noted by Dewar (1992, p. 158),

> [f]rom 1969 to 1971 patrolling was reactive rather than preventive. Battalions had some difficulty in even keeping up with the pace of events; they were seldom able to take the initiative. As the years

passed, however, patrolling maps were updated, and the sheer volume of intelligence on the inhabitants of the battalion or company area of responsibility provided such a degree of background information that patrol commanders were able to put a name to most of the faces they passed on the street.

These improvements significantly diminished (but did not altogether eliminate) British forces' vulnerability to deceptions—a success story in countering an opponent's deception efforts. As a side note, the IRA were not alone in employing deception methods to gain their objectives. Eamon Collins, a former intelligence officer in the IRA, related (1997, p. 168) that

> [m]y job in Customs gave me opportunities to drive around Bessbrook inconspicuously. I had spotted unmarked Sherpa vans leaving the barracks containing [British] soldiers in plain clothes, obviously involved in covert SAS operations . . .

HOW MIGHT URBAN TERRAIN HINDER DECEPTION?

Insofar as urban terrain may adversely affect the conduct of deception, it most likely sharpens the difficulties of using deception in two categories mentioned earlier, namely, cost and deconfliction. Discovery, the penetration by an adversary of a ruse, is potentially devastating regardless of the environment it occurs in.

While the employment of deception is never cost free, it may prove more expensive in time, manpower, and resources in an urban environment. For example, the close detection ranges, discontinuous color schemes, wide variation in visibility, and manifold observation angles found in urban terrain may require that camouflage or decoys be made more lifelike (and thus more expensive) than their desert kin. Or it may be the case that establishing a visible pattern (to effect the crying wolf ploy) is more difficult against the cacophony of city activities than in the stillness of the desert. These questions beg experimentation and analysis.

Urban terrain, in comparison with desert terrain for example, is a treasure trove of intelligence sources; SIGINT, COMINT, IMINT, MASINT, and especially HUMINT channels are frequently all available to combatants. However, as noted above, this glut is a noisy background against which to search for authentic signals. This probably raises the level of coordination and oversight necessary in the urban environment for one side to deceive the other successfully, as well as to prevent its own or nonaligned forces from inadvertently collecting and believing a deception story.

Chapter Five

CONCLUSIONS

By indirections find directions out.

—William Shakespeare, *Hamlet*, Act II, Scene I

It is a widely held perception that the post–Cold War world contains many possible Davids and only a handful of Goliaths (of which the United States is the most powerful). If history is any guide, Davids will nearly always seek to reduce the inequity between their own capabilities and those of Goliaths by adopting an asymmetric strategy. One possible asymmetric approach is to invite conflict on friendly urban terrain, in hopes of hindering the stronger, foreign foe. Chapter Two of this report examined how this may occur and the effects to be expected. Another possible asymmetric approach is to employ guile and trickery—deception—in the hopes of inducing the stronger foe to misapply those strengths and perhaps even expose some weaknesses. Chapter Three detailed the means and manner in which this is done, and the advantages to be gained thereby. It is the thrust of this analysis that the urban environment offers the possibility of using *both asymmetric strategies at once*, for cumulative or even synergistic effect. Chapter Four explored the potentiating interrelationship between the urban environment and deception.

Two policy outcomes have crystallized from this analysis:

- The United States, cast in the role of Goliath, must be prepared for the use of deception by adversaries during urban operations of virtually every sort. The United States need not follow in the biblical Goliath's footsteps and be brought low by an opponent's asymmetric approach.

- While it is true that the United States will most often be operating in foreign urban environments, this in no way precludes U.S. forces from employing their *own* asymmetric strategy to great effect, using deception to curb the advantages of future urban adversaries.

The first outcome prescribes important measures for U.S. forces: preparing—in training and simulations, in intelligence collection and analysis, in technological development, and in doctrine—to perceive and counter enemy deception efforts. In Charlie Beckwith's oft-quoted words, "You fight the way you train." This means that to resist deception on the urban battlefields of the future, U.S. armed forces must face deception at all levels in urban exercises and urban simulations. This is true for intelligence analysts as well, who should practice on discerning not just signal from noise in urban environments, but signal from *spurious* signal and noise. For both of these goals, experimentation is critical to gauge the costs and effects of deception use by hostile forces. Experimentation can also be a useful setting to vet novel technology, particularly new sensors and information technologies. These pose an interesting challenge: more information is not necessarily better information, and thus increasing the security and credibility of intelligence-collection technology is as important as increasing bandwidth. Cities of the world vary greatly in the technological resources present that may be drafted into use by combatants; high- and low-tech urban settings offer different backdrops against which to experimentally measure the utility of various forms of deception. Finally, doctrine—which articulates and distills the hard-won wisdom of battle—must also better appreciate the historical power of deception in urban operations. Service and joint doctrine on urban operations should account for the challenge of deception just as they account for other vital components of warfare.

The second outcome of this analysis engenders an objective for defense policymakers: prepare to counter the asymmetric approach of the urban adversary with an asymmetric approach of our own. Why should the United States cede the application of guile and cunning to its adversaries?

When advancing upon Berlin in the closing days of World War II, the Soviet High Command ordered the massive employment of deception measures in order to gain operational and tactical surprise, reduce casualties, and offset German home-ground advantages (Matsulenko, 1974; Glantz, 1989). This is precisely the model of deception use that this report recommends for U.S. forces operating overseas. As has been discussed, the force in possession of the city, with time to prepare and a friendly noncombatant population, gains significant advantages over an invader (regardless of mission). The use of deception by the invading force *may reduce those advantages dramatically* by misdirecting and confusing the adversary as to the time, location, manner, and other aspects of operations. This hypothesis needs to be experimentally examined and measured. Additionally, the United States possesses unrivaled advantages in emerging information technologies, allowing deceptions never before possible. In short, although a massive frontal assault may bloodily turn an enemy out of a prepared position in the city, if a well-orchestrated deception can accomplish the same thing without a shot being fired, does it not present a powerful resource to be tapped?

Anderson, C. (1983). "Abstract and Concrete Data in the Perseverance of Social Theories: When Weak Data Lead to Unshakable
Beliefs." *Journal of Experimental Social Psychology,* Vol. 19, pp.
93–108.

————, M. Lepper, and L. Ross (1980). "Perseverance of Social Theories: The Role of Explanation in the Persistence of Discredited
Information." *Journal of Personality and Social Psychology,* Vol.
39, pp. 1037–1049.

Arbeeny, J. (1990–1992). Unpublished RAND research.

Asprey, R. (1994). *War in the Shadows: The Guerrilla in History.* New
York: Morrow.

Axelrod, R. (1979). "The Rational Timing of Surprise." *World Politics,*
Vol. 31, No. 2, pp. 228–246.

Bateson, G. (1971). "The Logical Categories of Learning and Communication." In *Steps to an Ecology of Mind.* New York: Ballan-
tine Books.

Baumann, M. (1975). *Wie Alles Anfing* [Terror or Love?]. New York:
Grove Press.

Begin, M. (1972). *The Revolt.* Los Angeles: Nash Publishing.

Bell, J. B. (1991). *IRA Tactics and Targets: An Analysis of Tactical Aspects of the Armed Struggle 1969–1989.* New Brunswick, NJ:
Transaction Publishers.

———— (1997). *The Secret Army: The IRA.* New Brunswick, NJ: Transaction Publishers.

————, and B. Whaley (1991). *Cheating and Deception.* New Brunswick, NJ: Transaction Publishers.

Betts, R. (1983). *Surprise Attack: Lessons for Defense Planning.* Washington, D.C.: Brookings Institution.

Blum, R. (1972). *Deceivers and Deceived: Observations on Confidence Men and Their Victims, Informants and Their Quarry, Political and Individual Spies and Ordinary Citizens.* Illinois: C.C. Thomas.

Brower, L. (1969). "Ecological Chemistry." *Scientific American,* Vol. 220, No. 2, pp. 22–29.

Burnstein, E., and Y. Schul (1982). "The Informational Basis of Social Judgements: Operations in Forming an Impression of Another Person." *Journal of Experimental Social Psychology,* Vol. 18, pp. 217–234.

Christmas, R . (1977). "A Company Commander Remembers the Battle for Hue." *Marine Corps Gazette.*

Chuikov, V. (1964). *The Battle for Stalingrad.* New York: Holt, Rhinehart.

Clausewitz, Carl von (1873). *On War.* Trans. Colonel J. J. Graham. London: N. Trübner and Co.

Collins, E. (1997). *Killing Rage.* London: Granta Books.

Courand, G. (1989). *Counter Deception.* Office of Naval Research.

Cruickshank, C. (1979). *Deception in World War Two.* New York: Oxford University Press.

Daniel, D., and K. Herbig (1982). *Strategic Military Deception.* New York: Pergamon Press.

Dawkins, R., and J. Krebs (1978). "Animal Signals: Information or Manipulation?" In J. Krebs and N. Davies (eds.), *Behavioral Ecology: An Evolutionary Approach.* Oxford: Blackwell Scientific Publishers.

—— and —— (1979). "Arms Races Between and Within Species." *Proceedings of the Royal Society of London Biologists,* Vol. 205, pp. 489–511.

Dewar, M. (1989). *The Art of Deception in Warfare.* New York: Sterling Publishers.

—— (1992). *War in the Streets: The Story of Urban Combat from Calais to Khafji.* New York: Sterling Publishers.

Dunnigan, J., and A. Nofi (1995). *Victory and Deceit.* New York: Morrow and Co.

DuPuy, T. (1978). *Elusive Victory: The Arab-Israeli Wars, 1947–1974.* New York: Harper and Row.

Eagly, A., W. Wood, and S. Chaiken (1978). "Causal Inferences About Communicators and Their Effect on Opinion Change." *Journal of Personality and Social Psychology,* Vol. 36, pp. 424–435.

Ellefsen, D. (1987). *Urban Terrain Zone Characteristics.* Aberdeen Proving Ground, U.S. Army Human Engineering Laboratories.

Erichsen, J., J. Krebs, and A. Houston (1980). "Optimal Foraging and Cryptic Prey." *Journal of Animal Ecology,* Vol. 49, pp. 271–276.

Erickson, J. (1985). *The Road to Berlin.* London: Grafton.

Farnham, D. E. (1988). "Logic for Intelligence Analysts." In R. Garst (ed.), *A Handbook of Intelligence Analysis,* Defense Intelligence College.

Feer, F. (1989–91). Unpublished RAND research.

Fein, S., and J. Hilton (1994). "Judging Others in the Shadow of Suspicion." *Motivation and Emotion,* Vol. 18, pp. 167–198.

——, ——, and D. Miller (1990). "Suspicion of Ulterior Motivation and Correspondence Bias." *Journal of Personality and Social Psychology,* Vol. 58, pp. 753–764.

Gall, C., and T. De Waal (1998). *Chechnya: Calamity in the Caucasus.* New York: New York University Press.

George, A. (1972). "The Case for Multiple Advocacy in Making Foreign Policy." *American Political Science Review,* Vol. 66.

————— (1993). "The Role of Knowledge in Policy-Making." In *Bridging the Gap: Theory and Practice in Foreign Policy.* Washington, D.C.: U.S. Institute of Peace.

Gilbert, D., and E. Jones (1986). "Perceiver-Induced Constraint: Interpretations of Self-Generated Reality." *Journal of Personality and Social Psychology,* Vol. 50, pp. 269–280.

Glantz, D. (1989). *Soviet Military Deception in the Second World War.* London: Frank Cass.

Glenn, R. (1996). *Combat in Hell: A Consideration of Constrained Urban Warfare.* Santa Monica, CA: RAND, MR-780-A.

————— (1998). *Marching Under Darkening Skies: The American Military and the Impending Urban Operations Threat.* Santa Monica, CA: RAND, MR-1007-A.

————— (1999). *". . . We Band of Brothers": The Call for Joint Urban Operations Doctrine.* Santa Monica, CA: RAND, DB-270-JS/A.

Greenberg, I. (1982). "Role of Deception in Decision Theory." *Journal of Conflict Resolution,* Vol. 26, No. 1, pp. 139–156.

Greenberg, L., S. Goodman, and K. Soo Hoo (1999). *Information Warfare and International Law.* Washington, D.C.: National Defense University Press.

Guzman, A. (1988). Interview printed in *El Diario,* July.

Hammel, E. (1968). *Fire in the Streets: The Battle for Hue.* Chicago: Contemporary Books.

Handel, M. (1985). *Military Deception in Peace and War.* Jerusalem: Hebrew University.

Harris, W. (1970). "Counter-Deception Planning: Strategy and Organization." RAND (unpublished report).

Hass, R., and K. Grady (1975). "Temporal Delay, Type of Warning, and Resistance to Influence." *Journal of Experimental Social Psychology*, Vol. 11, pp. 459–469.

Herek, G., I. Janis, and P. Huth (1987). "Decision-Making During International Crises: Is Quality of Process Related to Outcome?" *Journal of Conflict Resolution*, Vol. 31, No. 2, pp. 203–226.

Hilton, J., S. Fein, and D. Miller (1993). "Suspicion and Dispositional Inference." *Personality and Social Psychology Bulletin*, Vol. 19, pp. 501–512.

Hoffman, B. (1997). "Why Terrorists Don't Claim Credit." *Terrorism and Political Violence*, Vol. 9, No. 1, pp. 1–6.

Janis, I. (1989). *Crucial Decisions: Leadership in Policy-Making and Management*. New York: Free Press.

————, and L. Mann (1977). *Decisionmaking: A Psychological Analysis of Conflict, Choice, and Commitment*. New York: Free Press.

Jenkins, B. (1971). *The Five Stages of Urban Guerrilla Warfare: Challenges of the 1970s*. Santa Monica, CA: RAND, P-4670.

Jervis, R. (1968). "Hypotheses on Misperception." *World Politics*, Vol. 20, No. 3, pp. 454–479.

———— (1976). *Perception and Misperception in International Politics*. Princeton, NJ: Princeton University Press.

Johnston, T., and M. Turvey (1980). "A Sketch of an Ecological Metatheory for Theories of Learning." *Psychology of Learning and Motivation*, Vol. 14, pp. 147–205.

Kahneman, D., and A. Tversky (1983). "Choices, Values, Frames." *American Psychologist*, Vol. 39, No. 4, pp. 341–350.

Kelley, H. (1973). "The Processes of Causal Attribution." *American Psychologist*, Vol. 28, pp. 107–128.

Koehler, D. (1991). "Explanation, Imagination, and Confidence in Judgement." *Psychological Bulletin*, Vol. 110, pp. 499–519.

Kruglanski, A. (1987). "Motivation Effects in the Social Comparison of Opinions." *Journal of Personality and Social Psychology,* Vol. 53, pp. 834–842.

Lambert, D. R. (1987). *A Cognitive Model for the Exposition of Human Deception and Counterdeception.* Washington, D.C.: Naval Materiel Command, NOSC TR 1076.

Lieven, A. (1998). *Chechnya: Tombstone of Russian Power.* New Haven, CT: Yale University Press.

Lloyd, J. (1975). "Aggressive Mimicry in Photuris Fireflies: Signal Repertoires by Femmes Fatales." *Science,* Vol. 187, pp. 452–453.

Lloyd, M. (1997). *The Art of Military Deception.* London: Leo Cooper.

Marighella, C. (1968). "Mini-Manual of the Urban Guerrilla." In R. Moss (ed.), *Urban Guerrilla Warfare,* London: Adelphi Papers No. 79.

Mathtech, Inc. (1980). *Deception: Fact and Folklore.* Washington, D.C.: Central Intelligence Agency.

Matsulenko, V. (1974). "Operativnaya maskirovka voisk v kontranastuplenii pod Stalingradom" [Operational Maskirovka of Forces at Stalingrad]. *VIZh,* No. 1, January.

McCleskey, E. (1991). *Applying Deception to Special Operations Direct Action Missions.* Defense Intelligence College.

McCormick, G. (1990). *The Shining Path and the Future of Peru.* Santa Monica, CA: RAND, R-3781-DOS/OSD.

——— (1992). *From the Sierra to the Cities: The Urban Campaign of the Shining Path.* Santa Monica, CA: RAND, R-4150-USDP.

McGuire, W., and D. Papageorgis (1962). "Effectiveness of Forewarning in Developing Resistance to Persuasion." *Public Opinion Quarterly,* Vol. 26, pp. 24–34.

McLachlan, D. (1968). *Room 39.* New York: Atheneum.

McLaurin, R. D., and L. W. Snider (1982). *Recent Military Operations in Urban Terrain.* Aberdeen Proving Ground: U.S. Army Human Engineering Laboratories.

Menzel, E. (1974). "A Group of Young Chimpanzees in a One-Acre Field." In A. Schrier and F. Stollnitz (eds.), *Behavior of Nonhuman Primates,* Vol. 5. New York: Academic Press.

Miller, J. (1980). "Urban Terrorism in Uruguay: The Tupamaros." In B. O'Neill, W. Heaton, and D. Alberts (eds.), *Insurgency in the Modern World.* Boulder, CO: Westview Press.

Mitchell, R. (1986). "A Framework for Discussing Deception." In R. Mitchell and N. Thompson (eds.), *Deception: Perspectives on Human and Nonhuman Deceit.* New York: SUNY Press.

Monmonier, M. (1996). *How To Lie With Maps.* Chicago: University of Chicago Press.

Morris, M. (1986). "Large Scale Deceit: Deception by Captive Elephants?" In R. Mitchell and N. Thompson (eds.), *Deception: Perspectives on Human and Nonhuman Deceit.* New York: SUNY Press.

New York Times (1999). "Serb Is Killed in Gun Battle With Marines." June 23.

——— (1999). "Damage to Serb Military Less Than Expected." June 27.

O'Neill, B., W. Heaton, and D. Alberts (eds.) (1980). *Insurgency in the Modern World.* Boulder, CO: Westview Press.

Owen, D. (1980). *Camouflage and Mimicry.* Chicago: University of Chicago Press.

Papageorgis, D. (1968). "Warning and Persuasion." *Psychological Bulletin,* Vol. 70, pp. 271–282.

Petty, R., and J. Cacciopo (1977). "Forewarning, Cognitive Responding, and Resistance to Persuasion." *Journal of Personality and Social Psychology,* Vol. 35, pp. 645–655.

Rapoport, D. (1997). "To Claim or Not To Claim; That Is the Question—Always!" *Terrorism and Political Violence,* Vol. 9, No. 1, pp. 11–17.

Ross, L., and C. Anderson (1982). "Shortcomings in Attribution Processes: On the Origins and Maintenance of Erroneous Social Judgements." In D. Kahneman, P. Slovic, and A. Tversky (eds.),.*Judgement Under Uncertainty: Heuristics and Biases.* New York: Cambridge University Press.

Schecter, G., and D. Farrar (1983). *Camouflage in Built-Up Areas.* McLean Research Center. DTIC ADB074334.

Schul, Y. (1993). "When Warning Succeeds: The Effect of Warning on Success of Ignoring Invalid Information." *Journal of Experimental Social Psychology,* Vol. 29, pp. 42–62.

———, and E. Burnstein (1985). "When Discounting Fails: Conditions Under Which Individuals Use Discredited Information in Making a Judgement." *Journal of Personality and Social Psychology,* Vol. 49, pp. 894–903.

———, ———, and A. Bardi (1996). "Dealing with Deceptions That Are Difficult to Detect: Encoding and Judgement as a Function of Preparing to Receive Invalid Information." *Journal of Experimental Social Psychology,* Vol. 32, pp. 228–253.

———, ———, and J. Martinez (1983). "The Informational Basis of Social Judgements: Under What Conditions Are Inconsistent Traits Processed as Easily as Consistent Ones?" *European Journal of Social Psychology,* Vol. 13, pp. 143–151.

———, and D. Mazursky (1990). "Conditions Facilitating Successful Discounting in Consumer Decision-Making." *Journal of Consumer Research,* Vol. 16, pp. 442–451.

Sendero Luminoso Document (1982). *Desarollemos la Guerra de Guerrillas.*

Sendero Luminoso Document (1987). *Bases de Discusión.*

Sendero Luminoso Document (1988). *Documentos Fundamentales.*

Slatkin, M., and J. Maynard Smith (1979). "Models of Coevolution." Quantitative Review of Biology, Vol. 54, pp. 233–263.

Snyder, M., and E. Jones (1974). "Attitude Attribution When Behavior Is Constrained." *Journal of Experimental Social Psychology*, Vol. 10, pp. 585–600.

Stanley, R. (1998). *To Fool a Glass Eye: Camouflage Versus Photoreconnaissance in World War II.* Washington, D.C.: Smithsonian Press.

Stebbins, R. (1975). "Putting People On: Deception of Our Fellow Man in Everyday Life." *Sociology and Social Research*, Vol. 59, No. 3, pp. 189–200.

Taw, J., and B. Hoffman (1994). *The Urbanization of Insurgency: The Potential Challenge to U.S. Army Operations.* Santa Monica, CA: RAND, MR-398-A.

Tetlock, P., R. Peterson, C. McGuire, S. Chang, and P. Feld (1992). "Assessing Political Group Dynamics: A Test of the Groupthink Model." *Journal of Personality and Social Psychology*, Vol. 63, No. 3, pp. 403–425.

Thomas, T. (1997). *The Caucasus Conflict and Russian Security: The Russian Armed Forces Confront Chechnya*, Vols. I, II, III. Fort Leavenworth, KS: U.S. Army Foreign Military Studies Office.

Tversky, A., and D. Kahneman (1971). "The Belief in the Law of Small Numbers." *Psychological Bulletin*, Vol. 76, pp. 105–110.

—— and —— (1974). "Judgment Under Uncertainty: Heuristics and Biases." *Science*, Vol. 185, pp. 41–57.

U.S. Army (1988). *Battlefield Deception*, Field Manual 90-2.

U.S. Joint Chiefs of Staff (1994). *Joint Doctrine for Military Deception*, Joint Pub 3-58.

U.S. Joint Chiefs of Staff (1996). *Joint Doctrine for Command and Control Warfare*, Joint Pub 3-13.1.

Whaley, B. (1969). *Stratagem: Deception and Surprise in War.* Cambridge: MIT Center for International Studies.

——— (1982). "Toward a General Theory of Deception." In J. Gooch and A. Perlmutter (eds.), *Military Deception and Strategic Surprise.* London: Frank Cass.

Whelan, W. (1990–1992). Unpublished RAND research.

Wickler, W. (1968). *Mimicry in Plants and Animals.* New York: McGraw-Hill.

Wohlstetter, R. (1962). *Pearl Harbor: Warning and Decision.* Palo Alto, CA: Stanford University Press.

——— (1965). "Cuba and Pearl Harbor: Hindsight and Foresight." *Foreign Affairs,* July.

——— (1979). "The Pleasures of Self-Deception." *Washington Quarterly,* Autumn, pp. 54–63.